René Hubert

The Man Who Dressed Film Stars and Airplanes

Edited by
Andres Janser

René Hubert

The Man Who Dressed Film Stars and Airplanes

Lars Müller Publishers

8 Transatlantic Glamour
Andres Janser

38 Timeline

42 Gloria Swanson: The Greatest Star and Her *Créateur*
Elisabeth Bronfen

56 Designs for the Personal Wardrobe

68 René Hubert: Dressing Hollywood
Deborah Nadoolman Landis

78 Film Costumes from Four Decades

98 Time Traveling across the Channel: Hubert, Korda and London Films
Amy Sargeant

108 Look Back and Look Ahead

124 Photographs from the Studio: On Costume Photography as a Work and Marketing Tool
Roland Fischer-Briand

134 Costumes in Ektachrome

150 René Hubert and the Stage
Angelo Luerti

160 New York – Paris – Berlin – London – Los Angeles

180 "Our Famous Countryman": René Hubert and Fashion
Katharina Tietze

188 Fabrics and Dresses

208 Taking Off into the Jet Age: Corporate Design for Swissair
Andres Janser

220 Final Designs

232 Appendix

“What was Hollywood’s great dream? A fantastic world at its time. With lots of glamour and wonderful costumes and magnificent dresses. And what did that require? A lot of work – and a lot of money.”

René Hubert, 1975

Transatlantic Glamour

Andres Janser

Transforming individuals into characters: few on either side of the Atlantic have done this as exquisitely as the costume designer René Hubert (1895–1976). From black-and-white silent films in the 1920s to the saturated colors of wide formats in the 1950s, the multitalented designer shaped some 200 cinematic films and approximately fifty stage productions. Apparently without effort he moved between his native Switzerland, large European cities and Hollywood.

Hubert's trademarks were opulence and glamour: with his flair for lines, colors and sophisticated combinations of materials, he increased the stars' market value by making them look stunning on screen. He also designed dresses for the private wardrobes of Gloria Swanson and Marlene Dietrich with the same goal. Some of his costumes were made specifically with the star's personality in mind, while others gave a character a visual and physical appearance based on a screenplay and were worked out in discussions with the producer or director, regardless of the individual.

Born René Huber, his talent as a draftsman enabled him to gain an education as an embroidery designer in St. Gallen. He was not satisfied with the job, so despite his parents' initial disapproval he went to Paris in 1916 to study painting at the École des Beaux-Arts and later at the private Académie Colarossi. As René Hubert – the final *t* was added to his name in light of the French pronunciation – he began to put his knowledge of textiles and clothes to use, designing costumes for music halls. Preparation times were usually long, which made it possible for him to work on productions in different locations though they premiered at the same time: in October 1924 *Vive la Femme!* in Paris and *An Alle* in Berlin, in January 1925 *La revue trés excitante* in Paris and *The Love Song* in New York. In the beginning Hubert was sometimes not even on location, instead making his designs in Paris for use in other countries.[1]

René Hubert as a university student in Paris, 1916, photograph by Francis de Jongh

René Hubert after being contracted by Famous Players-Lasky/Paramount, 1924, photograph by Florence Vandamm

René Hubert's self-caricature in *The Paris Times*, 1924

Because he did so many designs for the stage and later films in Paris, Hubert was regarded as a Frenchman in France.[2] In other countries a signature such as "Hubert of Paris" proved to be advantageous for the production – and his career. In fact he became a US citizen in Hollywood in 1945 until relinquishing his citizenship after returning to Switzerland in 1952.

"Do You Know Gloria?"

Hubert's first film costumes were made for supporting roles in *Monsieur Beaucaire* with Rudolph Valentino and Bebe Daniels, which was shot in early 1924. Production of *The Humming Bird* with Gloria Swanson also took place in New York at the same time. In his memoirs Hubert dedicated an entire chapter to his first attempt to meet Swanson: "I wanted so much to meet this star and asked as often as possible: Do you know Gloria? As she was a great fashion leader that even brought her the unkind reputation to be a 'clotheshorse' that I translated to be a lady with numbers of dresses not all in the best taste. That made me very anxious to meet her."[3]

His efforts in New York were unsuccessful. When returning from Europe, his charm and linguistic abilities, and coincidence, worked together in his favor. On the steamship *Rochambeau* his deck chair was next to those of two Frenchwomen, one of whom turned out to be Valentine Petit, actor and wife of the director Léonce Perret, who was preparing to make *Madame Sans-Gêne* with Swanson in France. "From this moment on I just wait until Madame Perret starts to talk again about the new film and Gloria Swanson. Now I can't hold back any longer and ask: Do you know Gloria? Madame Perret looks at me, smiles, says: So you are also a victim of her charms? So am I. But I'm sorry, I don't know Miss Swanson yet."[4]

Hubert managed to obtain a dinner invitation from the Perrets. On the basis of the first designs later presented for *Madame Sans-Gêne* (1925, lost), he was hired as the main designer. After shooting in and around Paris was finished, Swanson took him to Hollywood as the designer of both her film costumes and private wardrobe, the beginning of his career in the film industry. In *The Love of Sunya* (1927) the first costume appeared with a distinctive slit, which became famous in Hollywood as a "Hubert slit."[5] He dressed Swanson for nine films until 1941 and remained a friend for the rest of their lives.

Gloria Swanson in *The Love of Sunya* (1927), photograph by Russell Ball

Of particular importance for the history of design is *What a Widow!* (1930). The US poster for this melodrama about a wealthy young widow who travels to Paris to find new happiness promised numerous costume changes. Hubert's designs for it went beyond the current Parisian fashion for use on screen. Working alongside him was Paul Nelson, of the same age, an American who trained as an architect in France. And so for the first time the European – or to be more precise, the French – modern of the 1920s left its mark on both the costumes and set design of a full-length Hollywood film. This early work involving reception of the modern on the other side of the Atlantic, including its narrowing to the world of the leisured class,[6] has been lost.

Berlin and Paris: From Silent Films to Talkies

In the years around 1930 the industry invested considerable sums of money in a search for internationally viable business models for producing and distributing the new sound films. Hubert also benefited from this, as he worked alternately in Europe and Hollywood during this historical turning point. After a number of films for Metro-Goldwyn-Mayer (MGM) in California – including *The Wind* with Lilian Gish >p. 14 and *Love* with Greta Garbo >p. 80 – he worked from summer 1928 to summer 1930 for both Universum Film (Ufa) in Babelsberg, near Berlin, and Films Sonores Tobis, the French subsidiary of the German-Dutch Tobis-Klangfilm, which had its own studio in Épinay-sur-Seine, near Paris. After that he spent a year in Hollywood, returning to Europe once again in summer 1931; Paramount Pictures also had a subsidiary near Paris since spring 1930.

Erich Pommer, who produced *Metropolis* for Ufa, went to Hollywood after the film's financial failure in 1926. He worked there for a year, for Paramount and MGM, presumably meeting Hubert during that time. In any case Pommer thought about him after returning to Ufa, hiring him to work on eight films in one and a half years. The silent melodrama *Asphalt,* shot in 1928, was a high point of German urban film ("Strassen-film") in which the street stood for the opportunities and temptations of the big city. Hubert contrasted the subtly sophisticated, often shimmering costumes of the experienced con artist (Betty Amann) with the everyday outfits and uniform of the honest police officer (Gustav Fröhlich) who fell under her spell.

An early masterpiece of German sound film was made in summer 1930, the operetta *Die Drei von der Tankstelle*. The trio impoverished by the stock-market crash (Willy Fritsch, Oskar Karlweis and Heinz Rühmann)

***What a Widow!* (1930, directed by Allan Dwan)**

Costumes for Gloria Swanson, Adrienne D'Ambricourt, Lew Cody and Owen Moore

Poster for US distribution

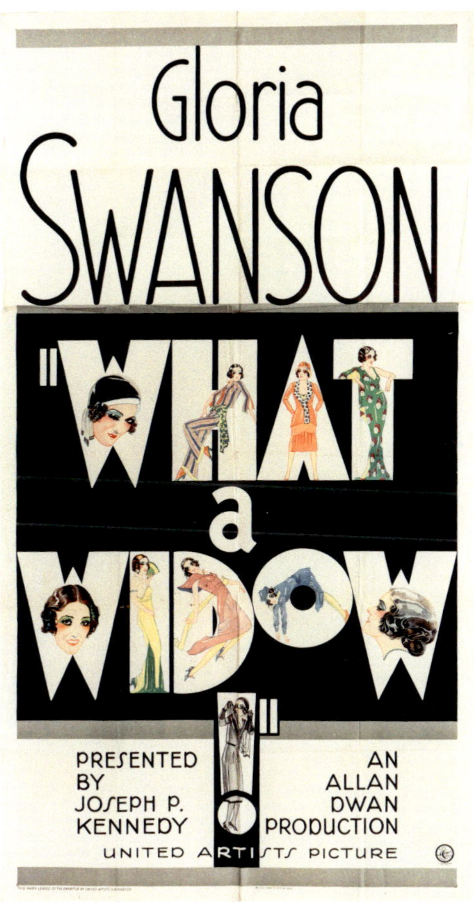
Gloria
SWANSON
"WHAT a WIDOW!"
PRESENTED BY JOSEPH P. KENNEDY
AN ALLAN DWAN PRODUCTION
UNITED ARTISTS PICTURE

Top left: Lilian Gish in *The Wind* (1928), autographed photograph dedicated to René Hubert

Asphalt **(1929)**

Betty Amann and Gustav Fröhlich

20 V

alternate between suits, service-station overalls and tuxedos. The light-hearted, wealthy Lilian Harvey prefers wearing light-and-dark contrasts and drives a matching sports car. Such graphic effects, which photograph well on black-and-white film, played a prominent role in two musical numbers in the film: Hubert's stage experience led him to combine various sheer materials and place frivolous white buttons on the black tops worn by the dancers. At the end of this phase in his career, Hubert even appeared on camera, in a supporting role in *Hokuspokus/The Temporary Widow* >p. 232.

A few months previously René Clair, the main director at Films Sonores Tobis, had made his first sound film, *Sous les toits de Paris* (1930). The light-footed drama about the street singer Albert (Albert Préjean) and the small-time criminal Fred (Gaston Modot), both of whom are in love with the attractive immigrant Pola (Pola Illéry) and wear flat caps befitting their class, was set in a modest neighborhood in the big city. Hubert's costumes carried a number of scenes: when Pola packs a suitcase before moving in with Albert, she puts in them the only two dresses she owns in addition to the one she has worn for nearly an hour of the film.

After spending the subsequent year in Hollywood, Hubert began working in Europe again in fall 1931, for Ufa in Berlin and for René Clair in Paris. In *À nous la liberté* (1931) the latter revealed prison labor and factory work to be essentially the same, and Hubert reinforced the analogy with simple, largely identical prison and working overalls along with sophisticated culottes for the female office workers. In a more stylized fashion than realistically, the lightheartedly critical satire on modern life became a model for Charlie Chaplin's *Modern Times* (1936). Hubert maintained his connection with Clair, shooting *Quatorze Juillet* (1933) with him in Paris, *The Ghost Goes West* (1935) in London and *The Flame of New Orleans* (1941) in Hollywood.

Most importantly, Hubert had by this point, at the age of 36, achieved the status of head designer for the first time – at Les Studios Paramount in Joinville >pp. 246–47. Costumes for the films, which were shot virtually around the clock, were normally produced by fashion boutiques and specialized studios.[7] In light of the unusual production methods, tailoring also took place on site: "We made the films in several languages all every time with a group of actors of their country. It was great fun and great work to dress all the different figures in if possible the same style as the

Die Drei von der Tankstelle (1930)

Willy Fritsch, Oskar Karlweis and Heinz Rühmann

Oskar Karlweis and Lilian Harvey

>*Sous les toits de Paris* (1930)

Gaston Modot and Pola Illéry

Pola Illéry and Albert Préjean

>>*À nous la liberté* (1931)

Raymond Cordy and Henri Marchand

Production line at record-player factory

French film version. But very often the Italian or Spanish star was so completely different that hat and gowns would look strange. So new folks had to be designed and made in a hurry, as the actors made the same décor one after the other – day and night shifts!"[8]

When all language versions are counted, Les Studios Paramount produced approximately 300 films from 1930 to 1933, two each week. In some cases there were up to ten versions, though four or five were usual.[9] Prints of most films no longer exist, as a result of which it is unclear how many Hubert worked on as a designer. About one dozen titles are confirmed, including *Tu seras Duchesse* (1932), *Monsieur Albert* (1932) and *Topaze* (1932). While these films were presumably less ambitious in an artistic sense than those of Films Sonores Tobis, they provided Hubert with an opportunity to show the range of his talents: "For a thin, modern, bright student with little money he designed simple two-piece costumes jazzed up with a white collar or an amusing tie, such as what Meg Lemonnier wore in *Il est charmant* (1932). On the other hand, for an attractive, coquettish Englishwoman with time on her hands he created extremely feminine clothes combined with black velvet and beaded embroidery, such as Betty Stockfeld's in *Une nuit à l'hotel* (1931)."[10]

After dubbing became common, the Hollywood studio ended its ambitious experiment and closed the Paris subsidiary. The National Socialists seizing power in Germany in 1933 made employment for homosexuals – such as Hubert – impossible, so he took the steamer *Paris* from Le Havre to New York on April 18, 1934.[11]

"Being Gay Actually Carried with It Some Cachet"

This was how the film historian William J. Mann described the situation that the majority of Hollywood's costume designers were homosexual in the 1920s and 1930s.[12] Their way of life differed for the most part from the values of the middle-class audience members flocking to see the films of Shirley Temple, which will be discussed below. In Berlin, Erik Charell's operettas had connotations that made them interesting for a homosexual audience[13] – an example being *Im weissen Rössl*, for which Hubert designed costumes at the same time as for the film *Die Drei von der Tankstelle* > pp. 170–171. Some of his shows in London were similar, including those with Ivor Novello.[14]

Hubert never made public statements regarding his sexual orientation. The discretion demanded at the time and by Hollywood's studio bosses

Costumes for Les Studios Paramount

Edwige Feuillère in *Monsieur Albert* (1932)

Design for Meg Lemonnier in *Il est charmant* (1932)

Design for Marie Bell in *La chance* (1931)

makes the chapter in his memoirs in which he openly writes about eroticism and sexuality in the early 1930s even more noteworthy. At the same time, however, the influence of editing for its planned publication in the 1970s remains a mystery:

"We all have our most brilliant, most lovable, most soul eating pet in our life. Well, mine is a Wolf! Blond, strong, blue eyed, devastating for male and female. The 'Zoo' where I met him was called Berlin. Berlin at its height of brilliance before Hitler, when the Kurfürstendamm was an avenue of flowers, the Hotel Adlon the aristocrats' adobe for fun and the Kleist Casino[15] the warmest spot of the metropolis. . . . The elegance of the smart nightclubs with telephones on each table – or the Schwulen-Dielen with 'Lederhuren' and white tie clientele. All was unique 'Zoo Berlin'! Girls with big breasts that swallowed any given number of firecrackers. Or boys that did not hesitate to oblige any size of unbottened [*sic*] uniforms. Well, Wolf was a Berliner, washed with all the Spree water and the French champagne that was flowing. That my scratches from its paws were numerous and exciting is to understand. And so were his touches, as wonderful from his soft real soul. You probably think now I was in love with him. Yes, I was! The girlfriend I had at the time fell in love with him! That made many things easier, and less painful – and more amusing!"[16]

In 1933 Hubert took his "Wolf" to Paris and later to Hollywood. The latter then continued on to Hawaii and Shanghai, and so Hubert lost contact with him. In the 1950s he met his partner of many years, Georges Stamatiadis,[17] with whom he lived in Zurich until his death in 1976.

The Costume as an Idol

Fashion helped sell movie tickets – meaning it was only a short step to sales of fashion from films. According to a note in Hubert's memoirs, glamorous costumes made for Marlene Dietrich and Vivien Leigh were sold in the United States around 1940.[18]

The largest numbers of his designs were for innocuous children's dresses made for Shirley Temple. Around 1935 the seven-year-old was Hollywood's top-earning actor, receiving a weekly salary of $4,000 plus $20,000 per film. Her parents were also successful at merchandising, earning an additional $1,000 weekly in royalties for products with her name on them: underwear, coats, hats, shoes, books, hairbands, soap, toys, cereal bowls and milk jugs.[19]

René Hubert with costume designer Adrian in Culver City, circa 1930

Curly Top (1935)

Shirley Temple with Shirley Temple doll in dress based on film costume

Shirley Temple and child's dress based on film costume, patent specification, United States Patent Office (1935)

Dec. 31, 1935.
R. HUBERT
Des. 98,038
DRESS
Filed Nov. 2, 1935
Fig.1
Fig.2.
INVENTOR.
Rene Hubert
BY Leonard L. Kalish
ATTORNEY.

Hubert designed costumes for only two Temple vehicles: *Our Little Girl* and *Curly Top* (both 1935, Fox Film). Temple was not the first child film star, but she was the first for whom clothes were designed and tailored specifically. Subsequently hundreds of thousands of these outfits were sold, supposedly four million in the case of one of Hubert's designs[20] – the price was twice the normal amount. His business sense even inspired him to patent a dress, with the justification: "The dominant feature of the design is the novel arrangement of the stripes."[21] Whether Hubert received a share of these sales is not known; the same is true of Shirley Temple dolls and their clothes, which were inspired by the latest film costumes. Temple continued to appear as a small child in little girl's dresses at the age of ten and provided a lasting impetus to the early commercial success of children's clothes.[22]

When Hubert was in Paris in fall 1935 for fashion inspiration, Alexander Korda, who also had worked at Les Studios Paramount for a brief period, invited him to London. Korda offered him a contract at his London Films, the most important British production company at the time. According to Hubert's memoirs, that was when he learned of the merger of Fox Film and Twentieth Century Pictures to become 20th Century-Fox, which voided his Hollywood contract. And so he accepted Korda's offer and moved into a studio apartment at 20 Chesham Place, away from Denham Studios, which was located outside London and close to the West End stages. First he designed the costumes for *Things to Come* (1936), the effect of which went far beyond the world of film, though not immediately.

Prominent shoulders underlaid with hard rubber and short pants or skirts dominated silhouettes that imitated the style of classical antiquity: the weather would be constantly warm in the year 2036, though the pants were designed to be shorter than the costumes used in the film. The film and its faith in progress shaped the style of science fiction films >pp. 118–21. Before then Forrest J. Ackerman and Myrtle R. Douglas appeared in "futuristicostumes" sewn by Douglas in 1939 that were inspired by Hubert's designs. This happened at the first World Science Fiction Convention, held during the New York World's Fair. Their appearance is now considered an important reference for the pop-culture practice of cosplay (costume play), in which fans wear the costumes of their idols.

Hubert's work for London Films involved numerous flights over the English Channel, as some of the women's costumes were tailored by the local

Things to Come (1936)

Design for 2036

Kenneth Villiers and Raymond Massey in 2036

"Men 1958," freelance fashion design, 1941

Forrest J. Ackerman and Myrtle R. Douglas (aka Morojo) in fan costumes she created at the first World Science Fiction Convention, New York, 1939, photograph by Charles D. Horning

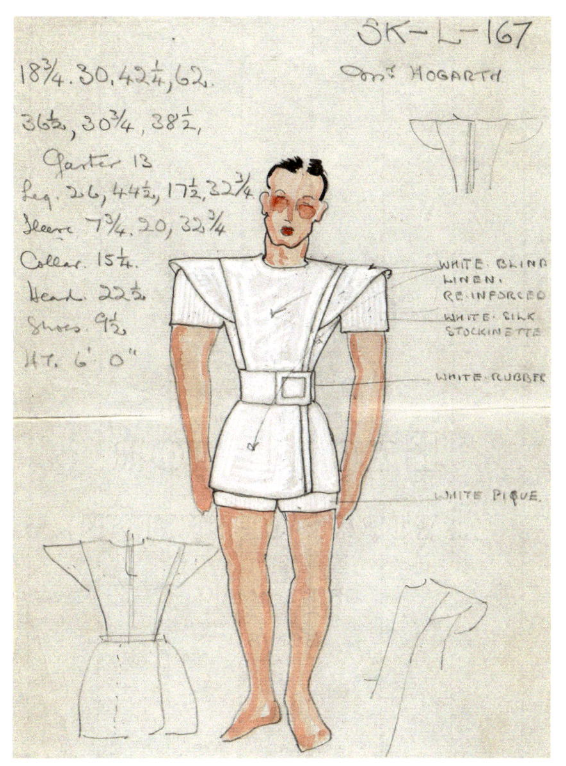
SK-L-167
HOGARTH
Garter 13
Collar. 15¼.
Head. 22½.
Shoes. 9½.
HT. 6' 0"
WHITE LINEN, RE-INFORCED
WHITE SILK STOCKINETTE
WHITE RUBBER
WHITE PIQUE.

boutiques Barbara Karinska, Jeanne Paquin, B. J. Simmons or House of Worth, while others were done by Balmain, Jean Dessès, Jean Patou or Schiaparelli in Paris – the customary source of the hats Hubert designed with especial care, made by Rose Valois.[23] He also enjoyed flying for personal reasons: "As I had kept a small room in Paris, I went many weekends with that then new airline that had those small fast airplanes to Paris to see my friends, some new plays or to fly the kite. Anyway, I was always back to London by the early Monday morning flight."[24]

Color on the Stage

The costumes for Paris music halls that Hubert had begun designing while studying painting were soon followed by work for stages in New York and Berlin. As a trained draftsman he put his ideas on paper himself, while others needed the assistance of illustrators. Of the thousands of color drawings he made over decades, several hundred have survived >pp. 161–73.

While the effect of the costumes' color was immediate on stage, it photographed as shades of gray in black-and-white films. This changed when color film became more common after the late 1930s. In theaters the audience can see the characters from different angles, not only the camera's perspective. However, in the spectacular revues, operettas and shows that Hubert typically worked on at the time, the overall appearance was normally more important than individual characters and often the plot – a result of the theaters' size, such as that of the Grosses Schauspielhaus, which had 5,000 seats. In Berlin, Erik Charell credited Hubert for the costumes in *An Alle* (1924) as "Collaborating Painter" under the name "René Hubert, Paris." This was the first official acknowledgment of his core competence, the visual, in Germany.

Unfortunately there are no photographs of Hubert's early stage designs after they were produced. The formal language of his drawings from these beginning years was indebted to Art Deco, and they were not suitable to be worn on the street due to their style – furthermore, they often revealed more of the body than they concealed. For the operetta *Im weissen Rössl* (1930), which is set in Austria's rustic Salzkammergut, Hubert was consulted for certain scenes as a specialist in contemporary urban clothing >pp. 170–71.

For Hubert's work in Britain, on films for Alexander Korda and also operettas and musicals in London's West End, more documentation

Earliest surviving film costume by René Hubert, Gloria Swanson in *What a Widow!* (1930) and color detail

"Mufftrick Camisole," probably designed for Berlin costume company Hugo Baruch & Cie., n.d.

Designs for operetta *Im weissen Rössl*, Grosses Schauspielhaus, Berlin (1930)

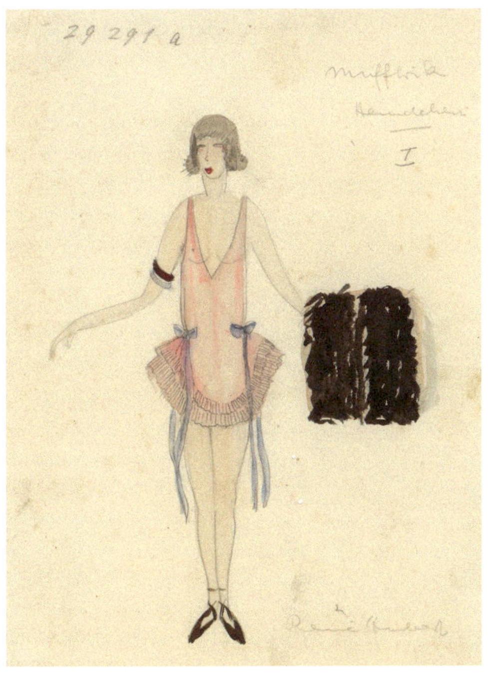

29 291 a

is available: the archive of the leading dressmaker's shop for costumes at the time, B. J. Simmons & Co., possesses dozens of Hubert's designs in addition to photographs of productions, though all in black and white, making assessment of the costume's color difficult.

His first premiere, in spring 1936, created a sensation: in *Rise and Shine* (Drury Lane) with Binnie Hale, the chorus line was not dressed uniformly, as was common; each member wore unique clothing, in every scene no less. Though not out of the ordinary in Berlin, it merited special mention in London: "The remarkable thing is that Hubert has made no two costumes alike. This is the first musical show in which every member of the chorus is dressed differently in every scene."[25] This approach to design was employed in a number of stage productions over the subsequent years.

After World War II began, Hubert tried his luck in Los Angeles again. Among his engagements there before receiving a permanent contract at 20th Century-Fox in November 1942, *Jump for Joy* (1941) at the Mayan Theatre stands out >pp. 174–75. Duke Ellington's first all-Black "revu-sical" combined satire, jazz and popular dance with a wide range of social concerns: "It celebrated Black America – highlighting its lifeways, aspirations, and even its sense of style."[26] Hubert designed the costumes and also the set, the lighting and the curtain.

The last two musical numbers before the grand finale were actually fashion shows. In "Made to Order" a young man (Potts Jackson) orders a zoot suit in the shop of two custom tailors (Pans Ware, Skillet May). This was an oversize suit with wide, high-waisted, pegged pants and a long coat with wide sleeves and padded shoulders that had become popular in working-class neighborhoods and dance halls. In the next number ("Sharp Easter") the young man presents his purchase when decked out for an Easter weekend stroll together with the two tailors and other characters.

The origin of the zoot suit is not clear, but beginning in the late 1930s it played an important role in the development of the self-confidence among minority communities in the United States: "The zoot suit was refusal, a subcultural gesture that refused to concede to the manners of subservience."[27] It came from the street and was worn on stage for the first time in *Jump for Joy*. Two years later the style became infamous due to the Zoot Suit Riots, in which men of Mexican origin were attacked by soldiers in the streets of Los Angeles.

Opening scene of *Rise and Shine*, Theatre Royal, Drury Lane, London (1936), photograph by Stage Photos Ltd.

***Jump for Joy*, Mayan Theatre, Los Angeles (1941)**

Bassist Jimmy Blanton, bandleader Duke Ellington and singer Herb Jeffries standing in front of curtain designed and signed by René Hubert

Potts Jackson, Skillet May and Pans Ware in zoot suits

ARRIVAL
DEPARTURE

72965

THE ROCKETS
WONDERFUL SMITH
POT, PAN AND SKILLET

Showing Fashion, Creating Fashion

The frequency with which clothing became part of the plot, and how Hubert was at his best when this happened, is noteworthy. The wealthy widow (Gloria Swanson) with her many fittings in *What a Widow!* (1930) and the fashion designer Geraldine "Gerry" Trent (also played by Swanson) in *Indiscreet* (1931) were followed by the owner of an upscale fashion boutique (Vivien Leigh) in *Dark Journey* (1937), the purchase of a dress at a luxurious dressmaker's shop in the seventeenth century in *Forever Amber* (1948) and the meeting of the young Napoleon (Marlon Brando) and his first love (Jean Simmons) at a fabric shop in *Désirée* (1954).

When an attempt is made to steal an inheritance in *Anastasia* (1956), the repeated efforts to dress the eponymous heroine appropriately make visible the ambiguity of her character, an insecure woman of the people or the possible unrecognized granddaughter of the tsar's mother. The Hollywood comeback of Ingrid Bergman was shot in Europe, so fittings could take place at Balenciaga's studio in Paris. Hubert had met the fashion designer in Zurich's Kronenhalle restaurant and was permitted use of his studio.[28] The other characters' costumes were made in London, including the minimalist uniform-like suits of soft leather that Yul Brynner wears as the mastermind.

As a fashion designer Hubert first made custom pieces for the private wardrobes of stars such as Gloria Swanson and Marlene Dietrich. In London he had equally wealthy clients such as the Duchess of Kent, Countess of Dudley and Lady Linlithgow, wife of the viceroy of India.[29] At the Swiss National Exhibition in 1939 his many creations for the fashion theater showcased products of the domestic textile industry.

In Switzerland, *Film-Mode*, the quarterly special issue of the *Schweizer Film Zeitung*, started reporting on Hollywood's current fashion trends in 1941. Interested readers were informed that Hubert participated in fashion shows in California and had also begun designing textiles – presumably with the intention of establishing himself more firmly in his home country, where fabric manufacturers that successfully sold their products internationally were active: "Designs of costumes and fashion for major films and elegant collections in the United States led to a desire to create his own fabrics, which are the beginning of all creations. Fabric influences design and therefore fashion."[30] His collections for the St. Gallen company Stoffel & Cie were also prized in the United States, such as by fashion designer Pat Premo of Los Angeles. The great

Jean Simmons and Marlon Brando in a fabric shop in *Désirée* (1954), film frame

Linda Darnell and Cornel Wilde buying dresses in *Forever Amber* (1947), film frame and costume design for Linda Darnell

Hollywood costume designers Irene, Don Loper and Howard Greer, who had also begun working with fashion to a greater or lesser degree, employed Swiss fabrics and embroidery in their collections; Greer presented dresses with Stoffel cotton in 1955.[31]

After returning from Hollywood, Hubert also designed prêt-à-porter collections and his work was included in exhibitions. In the "Swiss Natives Abroad" portion of the exhibition *Das schweizerische Bühnenbild: Von Appia bis heute,* two of his models were shown, first in Zurich in 1949 and then in Bern, Berlin, Vienna, Salzburg, Hamburg, Düsseldorf, Munich and St. Gallen.[32] The show *Der Textildruck* (1950) presented designs for Stoffel, and Hubert himself once created the pavilion for St. Gallen's textile industry at the trade fair Mustermesse Basel (MUBA).

Most importantly Hubert now regularly designed aircraft cabins and uniforms for Swissair – a significant portion of his late work after 1950. As a frequent flier due to his career, Hubert was well prepared to create the desired combination of glamour and professionalism. Ocean liners were becoming less important, and Hubert presumably took his first transatlantic flight on February 28, 1947.[33] This was worth mention in 20th Century-Fox's magazine, that their valued employee flew thirty hours from Geneva to Los Angeles with Transcontinental & Western Air (TWA, The Trans World Airline) – with layovers, which were technically unavoidable at the time, in Shannon and Newfoundland and a six-hour stop in New York.[34]

Hubert's Last Films in Cinemascope

In summer 1949 some of the last films for which Hubert had designed costumes were made. At the beginning of the year Oscars for costume design were awarded for the first time ever. This suggests that the glamour of the new trophy was not strong enough to keep him in Hollywood. At the same time the repression of the McCarthy era began, which presumably helped persuade Hubert, as a homosexual, to leave for Europe after twenty-five years. In the subsequent years the studios' crisis became worse, and they gradually eliminated their costume studios. In retrospect it seems that Hubert left at the right time.

Of the four films he worked on after 1950, two led to Oscar nominations: *Désirée* (1954), for which he returned to California again, and *The Visit* (1964), which was made in Cinecittà, near Rome. Both were shot in the widescreen format CinemaScope, which Hollywood introduced to set

Yul Brynner and Ingrid Bergman in *Anastasia* (1956)

"Afternoon Tea Dance at Elegant Château de Madrid, Garden Restaurant in Bois de Boulogne," illustration for periodical *Sport im Bild*, 1922

Raincoats designed and created by René Hubert for department store Jelmoli, Zurich, advertisement, *Neue Zürcher Zeitung*, 1958

HUBERT
René

Création
René Hubert
Der weltbekannte Modeschöpfer und phantasiebegabte Zeichner von Theater- und Filmkostümen hat einen entzückenden Regenmantel mit dazu passendem Hut geschaffen, in welchem Sie das düstere Strassenbild unter grauem Himmel fröhlich aufhellen werden. Mit verschiedenen, bunten Mustern bedruckt ist sein Material, absolut wasserdichter Plastik, und neuartig sein Schnitt mit den apart eingesetzten Ärmeln, zwei grossen Taschen und einem Bindegürtel. Der kleine Hut dazu steht Ihnen sicher so gut, dass Sie die Regentage nicht mehr verwünschen werden. So ausserordentlich wie der Mantel ist auch sein Preis (mit Hut)
Fr. 25.-
Alleinverkauf bei Jelmoli,
Spezialabteilung für Damen-Regenmäntel im 1. Stock
Für Mode zu Jelmoli
Stadt + Oerlikon

it apart from television. The studios were producing fewer films at the time but putting more into the ones they made. Crowd scenes, for example, required more characters and therefore more costumes. The costume budget of 500,000 Swiss francs for *Désirée* may have enticed Hubert. This sum covered three dozen costumes for Jean Simmons: as young Napoleon's love, Désirée Clary, she appeared in a new outfit approximately every three minutes in the film > pp. 134–147. Hubert had contemporary evening dresses in mind and struggled with the rules of self-censorship established in 1934, such as with historically correct plunging necklines.[35] For Marlon Brando's coronation scene he created one of the most accurate film costumes of those years.

At the same time as CinemaScope's introduction, Eastmancolor replaced Technicolor, which required different shades for the textiles: "The widespread use of Eastmancolor in CinemaScope forced costume designers to adapt. 'After making about 50 films in Technicolor, I had to relearn everything about chromatic values,' [Hubert] said. Blue, apparently, tended to be 'erratic' in Eastmancolor and kill other chromatic values. Furthermore, shades of red photographed extremely dark and had to be lightened, while they had to be subdued in the past."[36]

The rare combination of CinemaScope and black and white gave *The Visit,* the adaptation of Friedrich Dürrenmatt's play *Der Besuch der alten Dame* (*The Visit*), its unique character. In his last film Hubert benefited from his extensive experience with the use of colored clothing in a black-and-white film. Her visit as a now wealthy righter of wrongs begins with Ingrid Bergman in white, and at the trial at the ending she wears black. In the rest of the film she appears in fabrics with striking patterns and observes the escalating situation in the village of Güllen at an elegant distance > pp. 198–205.

The film provides a revealing example of artistic differences between director and costume designer, limitations set by producers in the studio system. According to Hubert's memoirs, Darryl F. Zanuck, coproducer for 20th Century-Fox, approved his ideas and designs for *The Visit*, apparently over the objections of the director, Bernhard Wicki. "Of course, the director had no say anymore and put his o.k. on all the sketches. But he took his revenge! When I saw the finished film, he had Miss Bergman mostly all the time sitting – on the balcony, in her hotel room, in front of the dressing mirror – and all the very interesting and expensive gowns, executed with enormous care and love by Nina Ricci were lost. It would

The Visit (1964)

Anthony Quinn and Ingrid Bergman

Portrait of Ingrid Bergman for magazine *Epoca* (1963, photograph by Fortunato Scrimali)

Costume design

Film frame

CINZANO

have been so easy to have Miss Bergman showing her elegance, her great wealth which we put into the handsomely embroidered and dappled dressing gowns."[37]

Hubert was not only able to move effortlessly between the cultures of different countries and continents, but he could also navigate various genres and their specific requirements. The constant in his multifaceted and multilayered career are the films from the golden age of the studio system. In Hubert's own words: "What was Hollywood's great dream? A fantastic world at its time. With lots of glamour and wonderful costumes and magnificent dresses. And what did that require? A lot of work – and a lot of money."[38]

1 "Mr. Hubert has recently forwarded to New York his designs for Ziegfeld's new revue which will begin in about two months"; *The New York Herald,* "Personal Intelligence," Paris, February 2, 1922, p. 2.
2 Dominique Lebrun, *Paris-Hollywood: Les français dans le cinéma américain*, Paris, 1987.
3 René Hubert, unpublished memoirs (in private ownership). The unedited typoscript has seventy-five chapters and the working title *Sterne haben keine Schatten*. See *Neue Zürcher Zeitung*, "René Hubert achtzigjährig," October 7, 1975, p. 42. They were written after Hubert returned to Switzerland and possibly inspired by the memoirs of Gloria Swanson, which were published in 1980.
4 Hubert, ibid.
5 "René Hubert: The 'Hubert Split [*sic*],'" in Lebrun, *Paris-Hollywood,* pp. 206–207; Lyn Miller, "You Wear What They Tell You," *Movie Classic* (September 1935), pp. 40–41.
6 Donald Albrecht, *Designing Dreams: Modern Architecture in the Movies*, New York, 1986, pp. XIV–XIX.
7 The costume for *Madame Sans-Gêne* (1925) was made by the local studios Granier and Pascaud; see *L'Ecran Illustré*, 1925, p. 3.
8 Hubert, unpublished memoirs.
9 Harry Waldman, *Paramount in Paris: 300 Films Produced at the Joinville Studios, 1930–1933*, London, 1998, p. xii.
10 Suzanne Chantal, "Le roman d'une robe de cinéma," *Cinémonde*, no. 196, July 21, 1932, pp. 592–593.
11 According to the passenger list.
12 William J. Mann, *Behind the Screen: How Gays and Lesbians Shaped Hollywood, 1910–1969*, New York, 2001, p. 42.
13 Kevin Clarke, "Im Rausch der Genüsse: Erik Charell und die entfesselte Revueoperette im Berlin der 1920er-Jahre," in ed. Kevin Clarke, *Glitter and Be Gay: Die authentische Operette und ihre schwulen Verehrer*, Hamburg, 2007, pp. 108–139.
14 Richard C. Norton, "Mad About the Boys: Die britischen Operetten von Noël Coward und Ivor Novello," in Clarke, *Glitter and Be Gay,* pp. 171–203.
15 The Kleist-Casino on Kleiststrasse was a gay bar from 1921 to 1936 and reopened for a few years after the war ended.
16 Hubert, unpublished memoirs.
17 Born in Greece in 1924, died in Zurich in 1978.
18 René Hubert, *Biography of René Hubert*, typoscript, 1941, estate of René Hubert, Collection Cinémathèque suisse, Lausanne. Published in nearly its entirety as "René Hubert: Ein Schweizer – Modekönig von Hollywood," *Film-Mode*, no. 1 (1941).
19 Robert Windeler, *The Films of Shirley Temple*, Secaucus, NJ, 1978.
20 Hubert, unpublished memoirs.
21 United States Patent Office, Des. 98,038, December 31, 1935.
22 David Thomas Cook, *The Commodification of Childhood*, Durham/London, 2004, pp. 91–94.
23 Hubert, unpublished memoirs. The costumes for male actors were made by men's tailors.
24 Ibid.
25 *The News Chronicle*, April 28, 1936.
26 Benjamin Cawthra, "Duke Ellington's *Jump for Joy* and the Fight for Equality in Wartime Los Angeles," *Southern California Quarterly* 98, no. 1 (2016), p. 49.
27 Stuart Cosgrove, "The Zoot Suit and Style Warfare," in ed. Angela McRobbie, *Zoot Suits and Second-Hand Dresses*, London, 1989, p. 4.
28 Hubert, unpublished memoirs.
29 "René Hubert," *Film-Mode*, no. 1 (1941).
30 "René Hubert entwirft Stoffe für Paris, New York, Hollywood," *Film-Mode*, no. 2 (1950).
31 Helene Miller, "Schweizer Frühjahrsgewebe für Los Angeles," *Schweizer Textilien*, no. 4 (1955).
32 *Das schweizerische Bühnenbild: Von Appia bis heute,* ed. Edmund Stadler, exh. cat., Schweizerische Gesellschaft für Theaterkultur, Thalwil, 1951, pp. 33–34.
33 Passenger list of Transcontinental & Western Air Inc.
34 Lee Roth, "Ladies' Wardrobe," *Action* 8, no. 5 (April 1947).
35 "Napoleonic Era Bosom Display Not Reproducible Under Yankee Code," *Variety*, no. 4 (1954), p. 16.
36 Ibid.
37 Hubert, unpublished memoirs.
38 Tobias Wyss, *Film heute,* portrait of René Hubert, Schweizer Fernsehen, 1975, https://www.youtube.com/watch?v=6RVexVCv8sw.

Actor June Haver with costume designers René Hubert and Charles Le Maire during preproduction preparations for *Oh, You Beautiful Doll* (1949)

Selected Works in Europe

1921–1922
Paris
Costumes for music halls (collaboration): Ba-ta-Clan, *Théâtre de la Chauve-Souris* at the Théâtre Femina
Stage costumes (collaboration): Shubert's New Amsterdam Theatre (New York)
Work at various fashion boutiques
Illustrations for *Styl* (Berlin) and *Sport im Bild* (Vienna)

Berlin
Stage costumes for Atelier Hugo Baruch (collaboration)

1924
Paris
Costumes for music halls (collaboration): Concert Mayol, Palace
Costumes for Famous Players-Lasky/Paramount Pictures: *Madame Sans-Gêne*
Work at various fashion boutiques

Berlin
Costumes for the Grosses Schauspielhaus (collaboration): *An Alle*

1928–1930
Paris
Costumes for Films Sonores Tobis: *Sous les toits de Paris*

Berlin
Costumes for Universum Film: *Asphalt, Liebeswalzer, Die wunderbare Lüge der Nina Petrowna, Die Drei von der Tankstelle*
Appearance in *Hokuspokus/The Temporary Widow*
Costumes for the Grosses Schauspielhaus (collaboration): *Im weissen Rössl*

1931–1933
Paris
Costumes for Films Sonores Tobis: *À nous la liberté, Quatorze Juillet*
Costumes for Les Studios Paramount: *Tu seras Duchesse, Monsieur Albert, Topaze*
Stage costumes (collaboration): Folies Bergère, Théâtre Mogador

Berlin
Costumes for Universum Film: *Bomben auf Monte Carlo, Walzerkrieg*

1935–1939
London
Costumes for London Films: *Things to Come, Dark Journey, Knight Without Armour, Fire over England*
Costumes for Metro-Goldwyn-Mayer: *A Yank at Oxford*
Stage costumes: London Coliseum; Gaiety Theatre; His Majesty's Theatre; Metropolitan Theatre; London Palladium; Prince's Theatre; Theatre Royal, Drury Lane; Saville Theatre
Private wardrobes for Marlene Dietrich, Duchess of Kent, Countess of Dudley, Lady Linlithgow

Selected Works in the United States

1920–1921
New York
Stage costumes for Lee Shubert (collaboration): Central Theatre, Knickerbocker Theatre, Lyric Theatre

1923–1924
New York
Film costumes (collaboration): *Monsieur Beaucaire*
Stage costumes: Century Theatre

1925–1927
Hollywood
Costumes for Gloria Swanson: *Stage Struck, The Coast of Folly, The Untamed Lady, The Love of Sunya, Sadie Thompson*
Private wardrobe for Gloria Swanson
Costumes for Metro-Goldwyn-Mayer: *Twelve Miles Out, The Wind, Foreign Devils, Love*

1930–1931
Hollywood
Costumes for Gloria Swanson: *What a Widow!, Indiscreet*
Costumes for Metro-Goldwyn-Mayer: *Those Three French Girls, Min and Bill, Guilty Hands*

1934–1935
Hollywood
Costumes for Fox Film: *Music in the Air, Our Little Girl, Curly Top*
Several hundred thousand copies of a costume for Shirley Temple were sold.

1939
Zurich
Clothing for the shows at the Swiss National Exhibition's fashion theater

1939–1940
New York
Dresses and textiles for the Swiss Pavilion at the World's Fair

1940–1942
Hollywood
Costumes for various producers: *That Hamilton Woman, The Flame of New Orleans, Father Takes a Wife*

1941–1950
Switzerland
Costumes, dresses and texts in *Film-Mode*, the quarterly magazine of the *Schweizer Film Zeitung*

1941–1948
Los Angeles
Stage costumes: Mayan Theatre, Civic Light Opera
Hubert's own fashion label: coat dresses, handkerchiefs
Costumes for Marlene Dietrich and Vivien Leigh were sold as dresses.

1942–1950
Hollywood
Costumes for 20th Century-Fox: *Heaven Can Wait, Jane Eyre, Wintertime, Wilson, Lifeboat, A Royal Scandal, My Darling Clementine, 13 Rue Madeleine, The Foxes of Harrow, Forever Amber, That Lady in Ermine, Broken Arrow*

1949–1952
Switzerland, Germany, Austria
Costumes for the international traveling exhibition *Das schweizerische Bühnenbild*

1950–1966
Zurich
Work for Swissair: uniforms worn by flight attendants and cabins of the propeller planes DC-6, DC-7, CV-440 and the jets DC-8, CV-990, DC-9

1950–1954
Los Angeles
Work with the fashion designer Pat Premo

1954
Hollywood
Costumes for 20th Century-Fox: *Désirée* (Oscar nomination)

1955–1965
Switzerland
Work for St. Gallen's textile industry and fabric, fashion and shoe companies: Bally, Grieder, Jelmoli, Stoffel
Stage costumes: Stadttheater St. Gallen, Stadttheater Zürich, Grand Théâtre de Genève

1956
Paris/London
Costumes for 20th Century-Fox: *Anastasia*

1959–1964
Los Angeles/New York
Stage costumes: Radio City Music Hall, Los Angeles Civic Light Opera, Lincoln Center

1963
Rom
Costumes for Cinecittà/20th Century-Fox: *The Visit* (Oscar nomination)

“Gloria Swanson might not have been the best actress, but she was the biggest star. She had to look different every day, always elegant, always a star. That’s an enormous amount of work, but she was contractually obligated to the producer.”

René Hubert, 1975

Gloria Swanson: The Greatest Star and Her *Créateur*

Elisabeth Bronfen

A Self-Confident Woman of the World

René Hubert often remarked about Gloria Swanson that while she might not have been the greatest actor of the silent era, she was its greatest star. Born March 27, 1899, in Chicago, her face in particular, with her light-blue, oval eyes, long, delicate nose and inimitable smile, made her an icon of feminine allure in the Roaring Twenties.

Cecil B. DeMille was the first to recognize the potential of her sophisticated beauty, and he played a role in her breakthrough at Paramount. Her star image was established in three of his marriage comedies: *Don't Change Your Husband* (1919), *Why Change Your Wife?* (1920) and *The Affairs of Anatol* (1921). In postwar cinema she personified neither a tomboyish flapper nor a crafty social climber, representing on the contrary a self-confident woman of the leisured class who would not be convinced to abandon her idea of happiness. At the same time she soon became one of the most glamorous style icons of the day thanks to her lavish wardrobe. Everything she wore became fashionable.

At the peak of her career in silent films, Swanson traveled to Paris to appear in the US-French coproduction *Madame Sans-Gêne* (1925) as a washerwoman who knew how to get what she wanted at Napoleon Bonaparte's court. She was so famous at the time that a huge crowd gathered to greet her upon her return to New York. Gloria the glorious was showered with flowers, and she called it the greatest day of her life. Her fans' overpowering enthusiasm was a contributing factor in Swanson wanting to take control of her own career. One year later she turned down Paramount's offer of one million dollars per year and switched to United Artists. Gloria Productions, the company she founded while there, gave her the artistic control of her own star image she desired.

Sadie Thompson (1928), for which she received an Oscar nomination, was the only silent Swanson

René Hubert and Gloria Swanson, who wears one of his designs for *The Coast of Folly* (1925)

***Madame Sans-Gêne* (1925), Château Compiègne, near Paris**

Gloria Swanson in the title role

Napoleon (Émile Drain) introduces Empress Marie-Louise (Suzanne Bianchetti) to society

produced that turned into both a critical and popular success. *Queen Kelly,* in which she played the secret lover of a mad queen's fiancé, was shot one year later and became a financial fiasco. Concerned that the salacious direction taken by the script would not survive the censorship of the Hays Office, she had the director, Erich von Stroheim, fired and worked out an alternative ending. Instead of running a brothel in Eastern Africa, her heroine took her own life, inspiring her lover to show regret through this melodramatic self-sacrifice. The film was never screened in the United States and played a significant role in the end of von Stroheim's Hollywood career. Swanson's production company released just two more films.

The switch to sound films resulted in a downturn in her success over the 1930s. But her beauty, glamour and talent were matched by her perseverance. She stubbornly remained in the public eye, and almost ten years before her death she played herself one last time in the catastrophe film *Airport 1975*. To the end her motto was "When I am a star, I will be every inch and every moment a star."

Collaborative Conceptualization of a Star Body

Part of maintaining the resiliency of her star body was artistic designing of daily appearances, and no one provided more help in this over the long term than Hubert. Swanson met the designer on the set of *Madame Sans-Gêne* and then asked him to return to the United States with her. After that her contracts stipulated that he would design all her costumes. At the same time he also created the entirety of her personal wardrobe. Their working relationship was also mutually beneficial: while Swanson made a significant contribution to Hubert's international fame, he helped her be the world's best-dressed woman for a decade. The star and her couturier had more in common than just a similar fashion sense. His designs were made especially with her in mind: they fed into the star image, and in this wardrobe – and thanks to it – she adapted constantly to the expectations of her public and always remained true to herself.

The constant reinvigoration of her look was not entirely voluntary. Her producers obligated her to dress in a particularly exclusive manner and set herself apart from all other female Hollywood stars in terms of elegance. Her contracts specified the number of dresses that must be worn, along with their cost. An expensive wardrobe was vital to her star image. She and her designated designer, however, had control over this self-promotion. Swanson knew that her spot-on fashion sense could be relied on: she was well aware of what suited her and what did not. Later Hubert frequently recalled how she would phone him in the middle of the night after a soiree to discuss the latest "Swanson fashion." Inspired by her suggestions, he then produced drawings and accompanying swatches > pp. 57-65. The actual creative process took place in the subsequent exchange of their ideas. The end result was in every case a creation that was perfect for Swanson's body and personality, giving her appearance the appeal that a dress can produce when it has truly become part of the wearer.

In fact, the star's gestures and expressions worked so well with Hubert's creations because Swanson's glamorous appearances were based on ideas the two had developed together. She not only meticulously went over the script of *The Love of Sunya* (1927), which she produced, but she also instructed him to turn the world of fashion on its head and set the United States aflame with a deluge of fantastic dresses: "We have to dazzle them." The intention was to overwhelm the audience with both her acting and her appearance as a whole. Regarding the costumes used in this film, Swanson wrote the following in her autobiography, *Swanson on Swanson*: "The audience actually applauded when I appeared in a number of creations, particularly a dark sleeveless gown with jeweled straps and matching Art Deco jewelry."

In his unpublished memoirs Hubert described how much effort was necessary to keep the "Swanson Couture Salon" going. To better navigate the huge collection, he started a "wardrobe book" for her. Each double page had a color drawing that told the entire story of each piece of clothing and its intended effect. The dress itself was illustrated along with the accompanying gloves, handbag, shoes, hat, jewelry, wristwatch and handkerchief. Each sketch was supposed to conjure up its own scene, so that Swanson could imagine how she could appear throughout the day as the epitome of fashionable elegance. For this purpose the wardrobe book (which has disappeared) was brought to her bed the first thing each morning. While leafing through it, she planned that day's wardrobe and gave her employees a list of the chosen pages. Dresses for lunch, afternoon tea, cocktail hour and evening events then lay ready in the correct order and with the accompanying accessories.

Gloria Swanson in *The Coast of Folly* (1925)

Silent Film *Après la Lettre*

When Billy Wilder asked Swanson to play the lead role in his Hollywood satire *Sunset Boulevard* in 1950, she wanted Hubert as the costume designer.

Gloria Swanson
#95

Top left: Portrait of Gloria Swanson for *What a Widow!* (1930)

Bottom left: Gloria Swanson in *Stage Struck* (1925)

Above: Gloria Swanson in *The Love of Sunya* (1927)

Paramount commissioned Edith Head instead. But evidence of Swanson and Hubert's collaboration can still be found in a few scenes. Not only is it surprising that Swanson accepted this role, playing a fifty-year-old actor who is unable to come to terms with the fact that her stardom has waned, but she also decided to recall her own past career explicitly, including the time period that Hubert had created dresses for her. Swanson contributed portrait photographs and a painting of herself as props in the large salon of the mansion on Sunset Boulevard where her alter ego lives with her butler, Max (played by Erich von Stroheim). As Norma Desmond she is constantly surrounded by a forest of framed photographs showing Swanson's own past star body.

Wilder staged this cluttered interface between actor and film role as a claustrophobic density. Every table, every dresser, every free surface displays these haunting reminders of a lost time. Even the long table under the in-home movie screen, on which the forgotten star watches her old films at night, serves this purpose. Desmond lures the unemployed writer Joe Gillis into this crypt to write a script for a film about Salome, hoping that this role will be her comeback. At first he supports her foolish scheme, which has ensnared her entirely in her star body. But then he decides to pack his bags. In order to prevent him from leaving, she shoots him as he runs along the pool to the gate. A few hours later she strides down the mansion's staircase in a fit of madness, surrounded by police officers, reporters, photographers from Paramount News and onlookers, and claims she is still "the greatest star of them all."

Swanson's previous work with von Stroheim on the film *Queen Kelly* is given a new twist in *Sunset Boulevard*. To lure Norma downstairs, Max tricks her into thinking that Cecil B. DeMille is waiting for her in the foyer with his camera crew. At the same time the intense final scene attributes to the star, who has by this point lost all touch with reality, the same stubborn perseverance that Swanson was known for. Upon arriving at the bottom of the stairs, Norma addresses her butler, who is now surrounded by Paramount News cameras, as DeMille, the director whom Swanson had to thank for her breakthrough. Wilder permitted his female lead to rewrite the end of his script. At first Norma continues to play her role as Salome. She believes that the crowd surrounding her are extras, assuring them that working on the set with them is her entire life. She claims that nothing is

Gloria Swanson, René Hubert, Swanson's daughter Michelle Farmer and Robert Wagner at premiere of *Sunset Boulevard* (1950) in New York

more important to her than cameras and the wonderful people in darkened movie theaters. She then turns to Max, still believing him to be the great director of Hollywood silent films, and delivers the line that Swanson is now famous for: "All right, Mr. DeMille, I'm ready for my close-up." Before fading out in the film image, she makes sure to have the last word.

While Wilder reveals the disastrous consequences of Hollywood's star system in *Sunset Boulevard*, which depicts the destruction of the actor Norma Desmond through her star body, the choice of Gloria Swanson to play her indicates the many different ways she expressed her fame. In his memoirs Hubert recalls a four-day train trip from New York to Los Angeles on which he accompanied Swanson in the 1920s. A special car was provided, on the rear railing of which *Gloria Swanson Special* was lit up in dazzling neon at night. Like a politician crossing the country on a whistle-stop tour, common in those days, Swanson appeared at every station before adoring crowds who had come to greet their movie idol. Even in a small Wyoming town in the middle of the night, she appeared on the train's platform dressed in her pink negligee and a feather boa to charmingly smile at the ten or so fans who had gathered.

Hubert also remembered the dark sides of this fame. After Swanson had become the queen of New York's fashion world thanks to his creations, she could no longer shop without being recognized. When they visited Saks Fifth Avenue once, the crowd of women around her grew so large that they were forced to retreat behind a counter. At first Swanson attempted to keep her fans at bay with her famous smile, but Hubert noticed how she, a sufferer of claustrophobia, was soon gripped with fear that mass hysteria could break out. The two were eventually saved by a salesperson who led them to an open door. This was the entrance to a display window that was being decorated. They were forced to wait there until the crowd dispersed and they were able to sneak out a back door.

A Dress for Every Scene

Swanson also wore Hubert's costumes when transitioning to early sound films. In Leo McCarey's 1931 romantic comedy *Indiscreet,* the creation of her star body again relied mainly on these clothes, which were adapted to match her strong personality. In the same way as in DeMille's films, she played a self-assured woman of the leisured class. On New Year's Eve, Gerry separates from her lover, Jim, because marriage is apparently not in the cards. She wears a dark, sleeveless evening dress, and the only adornments are glistening buckles that fasten the two straps crossed over her bare back to the lower part of the dress. The costume's tasteful simplicity expresses Gerry's lighthearted self-confidence. She knows precisely what she wants in her love life and is not prepared to make any compromises.

Then Gerry appears in a light-colored, sleeveless terrycloth bathrobe while preparing for the writer Tony Blake's visit. She sits at the mirror of her makeup table, anxiously awaiting the outcome of this encounter, and sings a love song. The robe's ample collar covers her immaculate shoulders like a cape while she concentrates on her daydream, lost in thought.

In every subsequent scene Gerry wears a different dress that accentuates her mood relating to this romance. A certain accessory is given a special amount of attention: Hubert often commented that Swanson had a "hat face." Even the most outlandish millinery creation seemed elegant and fashionable when she wore it. And so Gerry keeps her hat on in the scene in which Tony carries her over the threshold into his apartment for the first time. The light, decorated border visually highlights her radiant face. She resists leaving his embrace, so he continues to hold her while she switches off one lamp after another. She had decided to tell him about Jim that evening, and after being gently set down on a couch, she removes only her cape and a single glove, thereby demonstrating how serious this is for her. Gerry keeps her hat on, as her confession amounts to a careful exploration of her lover's moral generosity rather than exposing herself.

The appearance of her younger sister ushers in the dramatic turning point, and with it a different costume. Joan has fallen in love with Jim without knowing about his affair with her sister. In the scene in an expensive restaurant, in which her former lover appears unexpectedly, Gerry feels she is in a tight spot. Suspecting that Jim's intentions in regard to her sister are not serious, she forbids him from entering into a relationship. At the same time she intends to keep from her fiancé the identity of the man courting Joan so shamelessly. However, Gerry is the one who bewitches both men in her glittering dress. Delicate, slightly protruding lace wings are attached to the dress's straps in such a way that she, when seen in a frontal view, resembles a shimmering fairy who attracts all light. Her younger sister, on the other hand, seems rather nondescript.

In spite of her warning, Jim sends out invitations to a celebration at his country estate to announce

pp. 51–53: Gloria Swanson in the final scenes of *Indiscreet* (1931); costumes shown in order of their appearance in the film

his and Joan's engagement. Gerry appears in an elegant costume, ready for battle, once again wearing a hat that flatters her face with a cheekily turned-back brim and playful decoration over her ears. She is bound and determined to open her sister's eyes. This eventually succeeds when, during the garden party, a salacious scene ensues in her bedroom. Jim happens upon her when she is dressed in a light-colored kimono and once again swears his love. Then Joan appears, and Gerry deftly slips into the role of the drunk older sister trying to steal her sibling's husband-to-be. Swanson truly directed this scene, which is reminiscent of her earlier appearances in melodramas she produced. However, Gerry fails to foresee that the man she truly loves would also turn up unexpectedly.

Tony also falls for her act, making another dramatic turn of events necessary so the couple can finally marry aboard the ocean liner on which Tony had planned to flee to Europe. The costume Hubert designed for this scene is also loaded with significance: a dark belt is fastened front and back to the light-colored blouse Gerry wears with a dark skirt, which accentuates the contrast of the parts' colors. There are two decorative buttons on the light-colored tab that drapes over the skirt in front like an oblong strip between navel and thigh. This detail cunningly suggests the sexual desire that motivated Gerry to run after her lover and sneak on board, then joyfully throw herself into Tony's arms. Of course, she wears another decorative hat in this scene.

Regardless of the extent to which Gerry's change of heart is reflected by these costumes, they most importantly underline the glamour of the star who embraced this role in McCarey's comedy. Swanson succeeds in looking just as she planned – in conversations with Hubert – in every scene.

Hubert designed her costumes for two more sound films, *Music in the Air* (1934) and *Father Takes a Wife* (1941). After that they remained friends, and he accompanied her to the premiere of *Sunset Boulevard.* A photograph from the time shows how close their relationship was. Swanson's hands are on Hubert's shoulders, and she looks at him with a great deal of affection. Her famed nose can be seen in profile. He looks back at her with an expression of devotion, once again entranced by her smile. He does not embrace her. On the contrary, it is as if the man's large hand spreads to underscore the silent communication between them – the *créateur* and his *co-créatrice* – which never ended.

References

René Hubert, unpublished memoirs (in private ownership).

Gloria Swanson, *Swanson on Swanson,* New York, 1980.

Tobias Wyss (direction), portrait of René Hubert in the program *Film heute,* Schweizer Fernsehen, 1975, https://www.youtube.com/watch?v=6RVexVCv8sw.

Gloria Swanson and René Hubert at costume fittings for *Music in the Air* (1934)

Gloria Swanson and René Hubert on the terrace of Swanson's New York apartment, 1953, photograph: © Fred Stein Archive

Design for Gloria Swanson in *Father Takes a Wife* (1941)

Designs for the Personal Wardrobe

Gloria Swanson's personal wardrobe
pp. 57–65: undated designs

coat about
arm lenghts
very full in
bak.
robe all
draped
very
wide
tulle coat
the tulle is
put on in deep
heavy pleats
on a yoke of
velvet.
very full tulle
sleeve
put on in deep pleat. too

belt
gray-blue crêpe
belt and cuff made entirely out of velvet

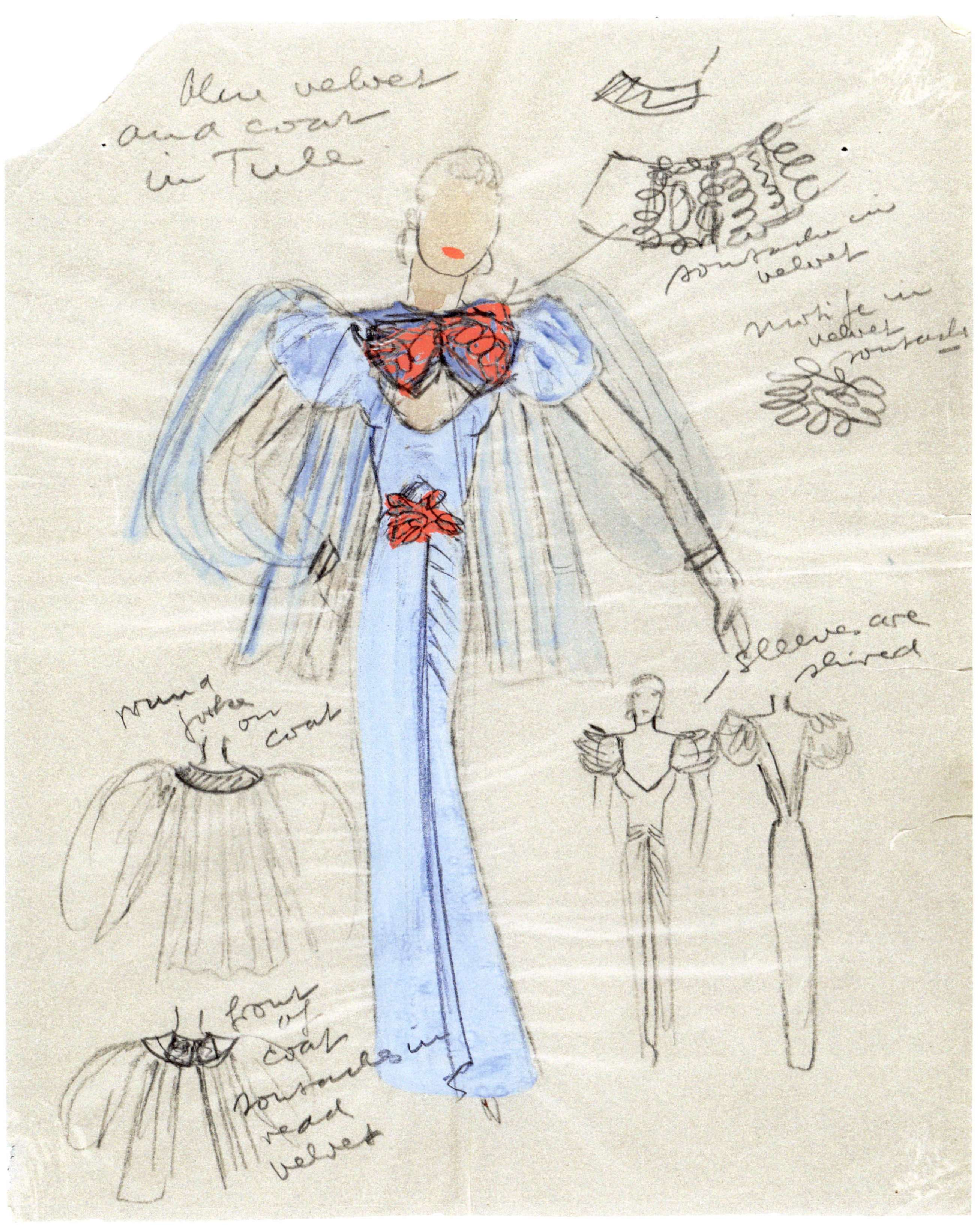
Blue velvet
and coat
in Tulle
sleeves are
shirred
round
yoke on
coat
front
of
coat

all shirred
silver fox.
velvet
Smaller drape which is stitched down on bigger skirt

beret draped very much to front
jewel
Soft gray wool
white kid in the middle
gray velvet on sides
Cotton velvet
back
gray velvet muff
gloves and sleeves all the same velvet

draped up
the cape is entirely draped up all around on too a crêpe lining
blue-green crêpe or changeable velvet – belt in blak patent leather
leaves in blak patent leather, stiched –
the stems of the leaves are in read patent leather – The skirt is very tight with a draped piece in front the panel in front is sewed on – the tight skirt (not loose!) and not full

draped
velvet sash-
seam where back
fullness begins
front skirt part
very tightly
draped
big hooks
and zips
in back in
white enamel
or covered with
white material
or knitting
the whole tight skirt is draped around hips
there is a seam on each side very much towards back
where the shearing stops – and the fullness of back skirt

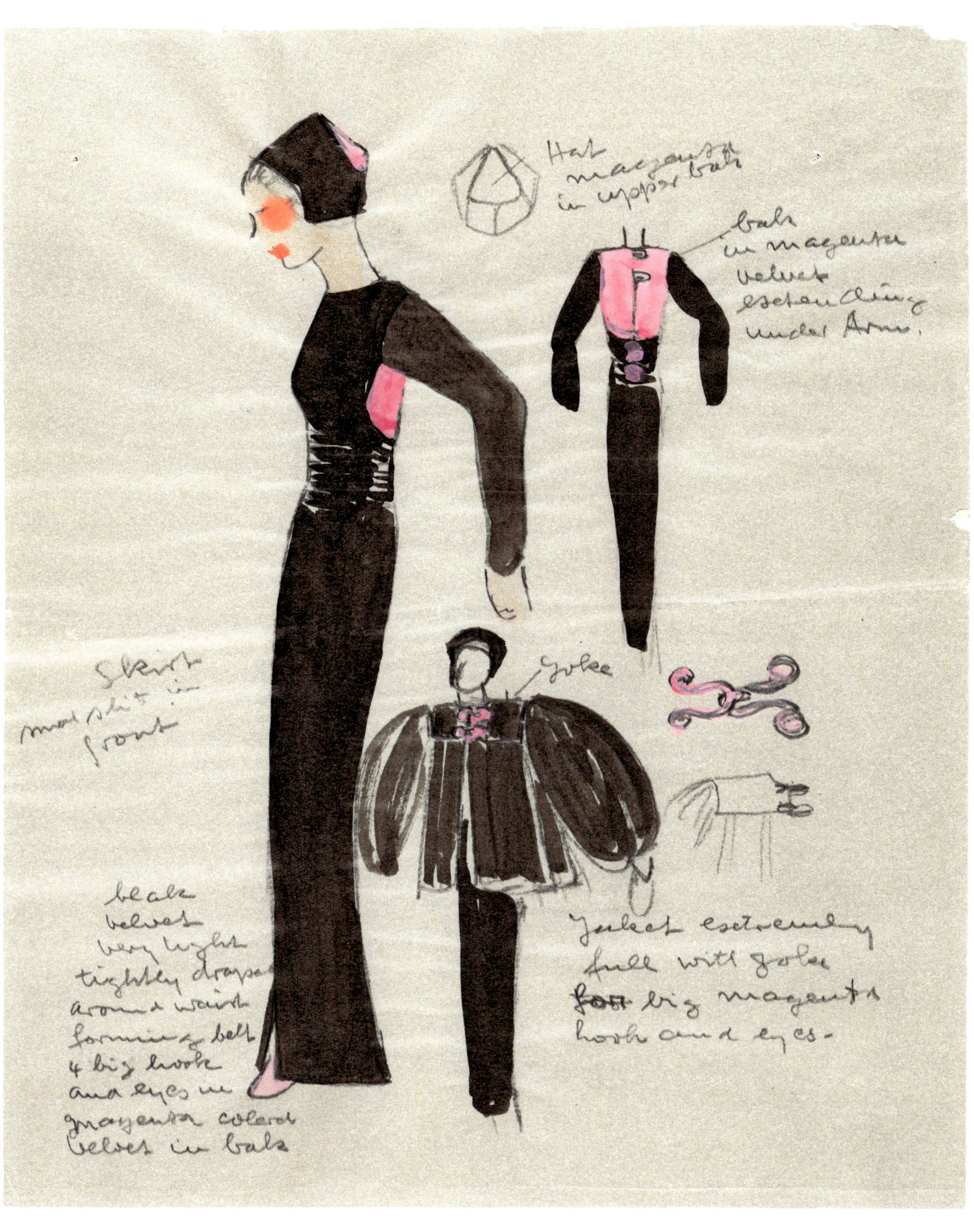

"Hubert and other costume designers had to please the actress, director, producer, themselves and a vast and voracious feminine audience. They were tasked with camouflaging figure flaws, staying within the budget, creating appropriate dramatic characterization and mimicking silhouettes for the period while … staying within the narrow censorship guidelines of the production code and designing neutral clothes that would remain in fashion until the film opened in theaters."

Deborah Nadoolman Landis

René Hubert: Dressing Hollywood

Deborah Nadoolman Landis

"We must create for the role the star is playing. We can't make her look like a fashion plate; her clothes must have individuality."
René Hubert

Born in Switzerland, René Hubert was plucked from the world of the Paris music hall by silent film superstar Gloria Swanson, which changed his life forever. Though originally sent to school to learn embroidery, he preferred painting, but after meeting Bénédicte Rasimi, a famous Paris revue producer and costume designer, he was hired to create sketches for one of her shows and quickly fell into the world of costume design. Soon he was designing musical revues in Paris for the Casino de Paris and the Folies Bergère, among others.

Monsieur Beaucaire (1924, costumes by Natacha Rambova and Georges Barbier), for which René Hubert contributed designs for supporting characters

Doris Kenyon and Rudolph Valentino

Hollywood in New York and Paris

The Shuberts offered him a job in New York contributing to their Broadway productions. There Hubert met 1920s matinee idol Rudolph Valentino and his wife, costume designer Natacha Rambova. Recognizing his prodigious talent, Rambova and Valentino asked Hubert to contribute designs for Valentino's great silent *Monsieur Beaucaire* (1924, costume designers Rambova and Georges Barbier), although he did not receive screen credit. For *Beaucaire*, shot in New York's Astoria Studios, Hubert was also asked to research eighteenth-century French court etiquette and manners. Later the press referred to him as "the outstanding authority of France on period costumes," which was noted multiple times throughout his career. So much so that, when designing at Denham Studios in England, it was reported in the fashion press that Hubert inaugurated a service to offer historical research for designers. He also signed a contract with Hills Brothers Publishing to write a book on period fashion, but nothing seems to have materialized. When asked by a reporter in

1938, Hubert responded that he preferred to design modern pictures.

In July of 1924 Famous Players-Lasky/Paramount announced that they would start making one film a year on location in Europe. The first film was *Madame Sans-Gêne* (1925). On returning to Paris, he was introduced to Gloria Swanson by Léonce Perret (who was directing *Madame Sans-Gêne*) and asked to submit costume sketches. Swanson was captivated by Hubert's sketches, recalling, "In every single one of his designs, he had underlined Sans-Gêne's character in the most tender, captivating way. He said that he estimated the ermine mantle he had designed for a scene at Fontainebleau might run as high as 75,000 francs, but when he assured me it would be unforgettable, I told him to go right ahead. I knew Mr. [Jesse L.] Lasky [Paramount studio chief] would love it." Hubert returned to Hollywood with Swanson and, for several years, designed all her clothes, both on and off the screen.

In Hollywood, Hubert was immediately recognized by the studios as a valuable asset. Metro-Goldwyn-Mayer (MGM), the largest and most prestigious studio, offered him a contract almost upon his arrival, and he worked there in 1926–1928, and again in 1930–1931. Actresses found Hubert to be a true collaborative partner. Lois Wilson, who met Hubert while working on *Monsieur Beaucaire*, employed Hubert's skills to transform herself from dowdy schoolmarm roles to the starring parts that she sought by turning the heads of her studio bosses in fabulous off-screen gowns. Hubert helped Wilson become a leading lady. With its impressive output of annual feature films, the studio had also hired costume designers André-ani and Adrian, among others, to clothe its stable of superstars.

The job of a costume designer was never easy. Hubert and other costume designers had to please the actress, director, producer, themselves and a vast and voracious feminine audience. They were tasked with camouflaging figure flaws, staying within the budget, creating appropriate dramatic characterization and mimicking silhouettes for the period while handling different color properties of film stock, staying within the narrow censorship guidelines of the production code and designing neutral clothes that would remain in fashion until the film opened in theaters. From the beginning of cinema costume designers needed to become experts at harnessing black-and-white film photography, using highly contrasting hues, silhouette, shine and texture for their creations. Costumes were designed and manufactured in color and then screen-tested. Crimson

Lois Wilson, autographed photograph dedicated to René Hubert

photographed black and pink appeared white. A fashion column from the time declared, "Hollywood, Where Widows Wear Red and Brides Wear Pink." During the silent era and the Golden Age, like now, setting a fashion trend was a happy by-product of a successful movie. When the audience falls in love with a film, they find the nearest place to purchase the clothes in the movie.

Like other well-known costume designers of the silent era and Hollywood's Golden Age, Hubert was called upon to forecast fashions and advise readers of movie and fashion magazines and newspapers on what to wear and how to wear it. Studio publicity departments marketed to the enthralled female audience how a particular costume from a film could be translated into the average woman's wardrobe. While Hubert promoted the costumes that he designed in the fashion press, he cautioned readers against trying to copy the stars because the screen clothes were too dramatic for the average woman and that "simplicity was the key." Often Hubert found himself the "expert" on women's fashion in Paris, Hollywood and London, comparing European and American women. Sometimes he would offer a barb-like "If women would not always look in the mirror and smile at themselves, the world would benefit by it."

Throughout his life Hubert designed period and contemporary films in various genres, including Hollywood's biggest box office draw of the Great Depression, the child actress Shirley Temple. Although he designed only two films for Temple, *Our Little Girl* (1935) and *Curly Top* (1935), they both learned and profited from the collaboration. Reportedly Temple overheard Hubert remark one day that "clothes for small girls should reach just to their fingertips," and from that day forward she insisted on keeping her dresses to within a quarter of an inch of the tips of her fingers. Designing for the pint-sized star may have been out of Hubert's comfort zone, but he invested the same care in the detail of her clothes. At a cost of $35 to $45 a dress, Temple's eighteen costumes for *Curly Top* were exorbitantly expensive during the Great Depression, when children's clothes could be purchased for just a couple of dollars. *Modern Screen's* fans were treated to a description of the detail that Hubert added: "The most exquisite handwork – little rabbits on pink satin pajamas, gay flowers embroidered on black velvet. There are hats to accompany many of the costumes. Even her shoes are made to order."

Shirley Temple in *Curly Top* (1935)

Cinematographer Rudolph Maté (next to camera), director René Clair (kneeling) and Marlene Dietrich at a shoot for *The Flame of New Orleans* (1941), photograph by William Walling

Head Designer at 20th Century-Fox

In late 1935 Hubert became head of the costume department, which he essentially created, at Alexander Korda's London Films. He worked out of the newly established Denham Film Studios and stayed until 1939. Never one to lie idle, Hubert simultaneously designed for London's most popular theaters and even designed hats for the London concern Teddy Thompson Ltd.

Back in Hollywood in 1940, he signed with Universal to design Marlene Dietrich's costumes for *The Flame of New Orleans* (1941). Since he had designed her clothes for London Films' *Knight Without Armour* (1937), Hubert was thrilled to work with Dietrich again. The lavish 1850s period costumes he designed included numerous layers of petticoats and a horsehair bustle underneath the six-foot hoop skirts, which were so large the actress needed to be taken to the set by bus. It would be his last film with Dietrich, but he considered working with her one of the high points of his career >pp. 79, 90–91.

Succeeding costume designer Earl Luick, 20th Century-Fox's wardrobe chief Charles Le Maire hired Hubert as head designer in 1942. A longtime fan of Hubert's work, Le Maire later cited *Madame Sans-Gêne* as the movie he considered "the all-time great" from a costuming standpoint. Le Maire created a home for Hubert at the studio at a key time during his Hollywood career. It was Le Maire's job to assign the films to the studio's designers, who clothed the female stars, and then delegate the costumes of the supporting players and atmosphere to the rest of the department. Male actors were responsible for their own contemporary wardrobe, a contractual obligation. However, for period films the studio would provide their costumes, which would be designed by the lead or the secondary designer on the production. Le Maire's position entitled him to a shared screen credit with his designers. Hubert designed ten films in just his first year at 20th Century-Fox, including *The Song of Bernadette* (1943), for which his deglamorized lead actress, a young Jennifer Jones, received an Academy Award.

Betty Grable was one of the studio's biggest names, and Hubert designed many of her films, beginning with *Sweet Rosie O'Grady* (1943), for which the studio ginned up publicity by insuring the actress's legs with Lloyd's of London for $1 million. Grable was the number-one pinup girl of World War II and an American armed forces favorite. She knew

René Hubert and seamstress at 20th Century-Fox's costume studio with the dressmaker's dummy for Peggy Cummins, who was initially planned for the title role in *Forever Amber* (1947)

her legs were her fortune despite her talents as a dancer and comedienne. She had not gotten along with Hubert's predecessor, Luick, refusing to wear his first round of designs for *Footlight Serenade* (1942). Hubert said that Grable hated making period pictures because it meant covering her legs, stating, "Grable wanted all long skirts made shorter and tighter, regardless of historical accuracy." Navigating the personalities of actresses, with all of their insecurities and whims, is critical to the success of a costume designer. Hubert's early training with the demanding Swanson left him well prepared to meet the challenge.

"Terrace of Club," design for Betty Grable in *Pin Up Girl* (1944)

When Supplies Got Tight, Designers Got Creative

During World War II, Order L-85 regulated the types and amounts of fabrics used for clothing in the United States. Costume designers knew that the American woman looked to the screen for inspiration and that supporting wartime initiatives was also good business. New York fashion designers complained that Hollywood was only paying lip service to the rationing, but fashion designers were more affected by the shortages of fabric and restrictions of yardage. Costume designers needed to create one singular costume, while Seventh Avenue had to manufacture thousands of dresses to stay solvent. Hollywood designers often touted their resourcefulness in the press; costumes were the ultimate recyclable, with studio costume storage overstocked with available clothes for remaking. For contemporary styles costume designers adhered to every restriction. For period clothes they either recycled or reused costumes from old productions (changing collars and trim). They also utilized luxurious fabrics purchased by the studio before the wartime mandate.

When supplies got tight, designers got creative. René Hubert stated, "Sometimes we made our yardage design by sewing small velvet pieces on solid-color material we had on hand. We even hand-blocked some of our cloth, and frequently we dyed an old dress a new color." There were plenty of times when designers had to improvise and employ creativity because of the limitations. A report in the press said, "The way Hollywood costume designers are cheered for the war's end, you'd think they had been dressing screenland's stars in burlap for five years. Designers, like the public, are tired of improvising substitutes for all the rich fabrics they used to get. The war rendered all European and many American textiles unavailable virtually."

Despite the restrictions Hollywood's costume designers found the resources when they needed to create the spectacular. Hubert created over 200 costume sketches for the biopic *Wilson* (1944) > pp. 84–85. The epic story of the Woodrow Wilson presidency included five major female parts, with each wearing between twenty and thirty costumes over a period spanning fifteen years. Hubert looked to French designers from the period, researching clothes designed by early couturiers Paquin, Poiret and Drecoll, from whom the Wilson women would have imported the gowns at the time. He also studied Wilson family portraiture and found newspaper clippings to read how journalists described the Wilson women's ensembles at important events. After the sketches were drawn, materials were chosen and approved by the Technicolor representative. All Hubert's fabrics were selected with (what he called) the "camera's eye," determined to photograph well. The long narrow silhouette of 1917–1918 was not in favor during the short-skirted and wide-shouldered 1940s. The 20th Century-Fox newsletter, *Action,* was relieved to report that it was "not a particularly exciting or becoming era for women's clothes, but Mr. René Hubert has managed to design some very flattering and truly becoming costumes without losing the authenticity and feel of the period."

For *A Royal Scandal* (1945), Ernst Lubitsch's tale of the palace intrigue of Russian Empress Catherine the Great, the producer was concerned that the tall wigs of the eighteenth century would overwhelm his actors' performances, killing the racy comedy. Hubert was able to justify Lubitsch's request after finding a book by a contemporary of Catherine II, who described a brief period of her reign in which the czarina rejected the French fashions of the period, including wigs. Although it was designed during the war, 20th Century-Fox noted that for the tale of royal intrigue Hubert used "a stock of pre-war materials the studio was lucky enough to have on hand" to create the regal splendor of the court, including voluminous gowns with hoops and panniers worn by Tallulah Bankhead as Catherine.

Bankhead was thrilled with the glamorous gowns, which sharply contrasted with the single costume Hubert designed for her appearance in Alfred Hitchcock's *Lifeboat* (1944). In that film she played an entitled newspaper correspondent, one of a group of survivors stranded in a lifeboat, who starts the film fashionably dressed, hair perfectly coiffed, makeup flawless, wearing heels and wrapped in a mink coat,

Geraldine Fitzgerald, Alexander Knox, Ruth Ford, Mary Anderson and Madeleine Forbes in *Wilson* (1944)

Hume Cronyn, John Hodiak, Henry Hull, William Bendix, Mary Anderson and Tallulah Bankhead in *Lifeboat* (1944)

her wrist adorned with a glittering bracelet. As the story unravels, so does her costume, losing piece by piece of the ensemble until she is left tattered and vulnerable. Bankhead called it "a striptease."

In 1946 Hubert signed one more contract extension with 20th Century-Fox. Otto Preminger asked Hubert to design *Centennial Summer* (1946), set in the nineteenth century. Although at the time he reproduced styles faithfully (with 1940s eyes), Hubert claimed theatrical license when he used brighter colors and "lighter-weight materials" because "actresses couldn't walk naturally in such heavy dresses" >pp. 92–93.

Toward the End of the Studio System

After almost four years of war (1941–1945), Hollywood was eager to resume production without wartime restrictions. Costume designers embraced all the fur and feathers, long full skirts and imported fabrics they had enjoyed during the Golden Age of Hollywood. Though designers got their creative freedom back, Hollywood was about to undergo a drastic change. The years after the war launched a new era in Hollywood: the end of the studio system and the rise of television. The repercussions that followed, for better or for worse, affected Hollywood lastingly.

During the war theater attendance was high, reaching a weekly figure of over eighty million by 1945. The year after the war, with filmmakers returning from service, Hollywood produced some of its best films, such as *Gilda* (Jean Louis), *It's a Wonderful Life* (Edward Stevenson), *My Darling Clementine* (Hubert), *The Postman Always Rings Twice* (Irene) and *The Best Years of Our Lives* (Irene Sharaff), among others. Despite the success of 1946, Hollywood's most challenging years were ahead.

Director Otto Preminger decided to mute the color palette for his 1947 Technicolor period production, *Forever Amber,* starring Linda Darnell and Cornel Wilde. Originally starring Peggy Cummins and recast with Darnell after shooting had started, the original costumes were modified to suit the new star. Preminger also collaborated closely with Hubert to ensure that his elaborate period costumes would not be overly garish when photographed in unforgiving three-strip Technicolor. Hollywood studios and their stars firmly believed that period clothes needed to be acceptable to contemporary audiences. Although the production code that regulated sex and sexiness on screen was still in place, actresses were eager to display more décolletage. Darnell bitterly complained that her seventeenth-century gowns for *Forever Amber* were unfairly targeted for their low and period-correct neckline, describing them as being “an inch above where anything starts to get thought about” >pp. 86–89.

In 1949 Hubert left 20th Century-Fox after seven years, although he was occasionally lured back for specific films that appealed to him. The collision of the studio system breakup, television’s rise and the desire for more realistic clothes seemed to alarm him as early as 1948. Hubert made his belief known that audiences had stopped looking to the screen for fashion inspiration. This statement anticipated the birth of television and the later demise of the studio system. He foresaw the fall from grace of the costume designer.

In 1949, when he looked back on some of his earlier films with Gloria Swanson, he noted that if he had designed them “today,” he would have been much subtler. He began to think of clothes rather than costumes as more appropriate for the screen and seemed to regret the early exaggeration of styles on screen. Remarking upon how if Swanson had played a salesgirl in the early part of his career, her costumes would have been made from the most luxurious fabrics. But, by the late 1940s, he was using the same materials her character would have been able to afford, even going to a shop to purchase something inexpensive. As the cinema changed and culture shifted after the war, so did the audience’s taste and expectations.

Each Star Is an Individual Problem, in Every Picture

While Hubert was working back home at a textile firm and for Swissair, his old friend Charles Le Maire once again approached him to design for Marlon Brando and Jean Simmons in *Désirée* (1954). The opulent world of Napoleon’s court hearkened back to his first film as costume designer, *Madame Sans-Gêne*. For *Désirée* Hubert reconciled the low-cut empire gowns with the limits of censorship and the production code (adding chiffon to hide cleavage). He also gave the clothes “the modern touch,” well aware that contemporary audiences could find these period costumes comical even with a lavish $100,000 costume budget >pp. 94–95, 134–147.

He admitted, “I knew little about that period, and then I did some research,” adding, “I’ve never before come across a fashion period where so little was worn above the waist and so much below!” Actress Jean Simmons commented, “René Hubert,

Ingrid Bergman in *Anastasia* (1956), autographed photograph dedicated to René Hubert

Ernst Schröder, Ingrid Bergman and Anthony Quinn in *The Visit* (1964)

the designer, told me that in those days the girls competed with one another to see who could wear the lightest, flimsiest gowns, and after seeing the costumes he has designed for the picture I know what he means." Hubert was delighted to finally receive his first Academy Award nomination (shared with Le Maire) for the film.

In 1956, 20th Century-Fox signed Hubert to design *Anastasia* with Ingrid Bergman, shot on location in Europe. For Helen Hayes' Dowager Empress Maria Feodorovna, Hubert collaborated with the venerable House of Worth. Copying an original embroidery pattern last used for Queen Maud of Norway in 1902, Hubert created the solemn but regal clothes for the empress in mourning. Without the speed and the expertise of the Hollywood studio costume shops, Hubert relied upon fashion houses in Paris and Switzerland, including Balenciaga. These couture houses executed his designs for Bergman's imposter to the throne, Anna Koreff. Bergman won an Academy Award for her performance.

Bergman requested the semiretired Hubert to create her costumes for *The Visit (1964)*, in which she plays "the richest woman in the world." In Europe Hubert relied on the fashion house Nina Ricci to execute his designs. (Ricci is also credited with designing other costumes in the film.) The film was his last. As if to punctuate the close of his film career, the designer received his second Academy Award nomination for *The Visit* >pp. 198–205.

Hubert insisted that he had no favorites among his stars when designing their costumes. "Each is an individual problem, in every picture," he observed. "Her clothes depend largely upon the role she is enacting. If she requires a period costume, we must consider authenticity and suitability." A designer must be a diplomat, too. Hubert says, "If they don't feel right – their acting suffers." Interviewed about the process and production of Hubert's *Forever Amber* in 1947, his longtime friend and mentor Charles Le Maire said, "The motion-picture designer, whether he creates the wardrobe for a spectacular film or for one where his work blends into a subtle mood or locale, is a vital part of every picture. I'm particularly glad that, at long last, he is about to receive the plaudits too long denied him." Although the work was often exhausting, Hubert enjoyed his time in Hollywood, describing it as a "fantastic world."

References

Earl Wilson, "Linda Darnell Hates Censors," *Miami News*, May 22, 1947, p. 31.

Leonard Lynos, "Eddie, Debbie Plan Return to N.Y. for Long Stay," *Salt Lake Tribune*, October 3, 1954, p. A15.

"War Rationing: René Hubert," *Dayton Herald*, October 31, 1942, p. N2.

"Amber Story Not All That's Toned Down," *The Washington Post*, April 20, 1947, p. S7.

Judy Jeannin, "Hollywood's Indifference to Fashions Is Deplored," *The Record* (Hackensack, NJ), March 22, 1965, p. 25.

Aline Moseby, "Movies Scorn New Fashions," *Eugene Register-Guard*, November 7, 1948.

Charles Le Maire, "Couture Important to Films," *The New York Times*, November 2, 1947, p. X4.

Lee Roth, "Findings from the Lady's Wardrobe," *Action*, November 1943, p. 20.

"Shirley Temple, Saver of Lives," *Modern Screen* 12/35, v. 12, no. 1, p. 78.

Sally Martin, "Hollywood's Charm School: Shirley's Personal Wardrobe," *Hollywood*, November 1936, p. 40.

Gloria Swanson, *Swanson on Swanson*, New York, 1981, pp. 232–33.

Film Costumes from Four Decades

The Flame of New Orleans (1941, directed by René Clair)
p. 79: design for Marlene Dietrich

Love (1927, directed by Edmund Goulding)
p. 80: design for character Countess Lydia

Quality Street (1927, directed by Sidney Franklin)
p. 81: design for Marion Davies

Wintertime (1943, directed by John Brahm)
p. 82: design for Sonja Henie for ice ballet
p. 83: design for supporting character

Wilson (1944, directed by Henry King)
p. 84: "Change 1, Hallway Tea, Meeting Wilson, Spring 1915," design
p. 85: "Margaret, Change 21, Scenes 258–259, East Room, Winter 1918," design

Forever Amber (1947, directed by Otto Preminger)
p. 86: design for unknown actor
p. 87: design for Linda Darnell
p. 88: design for Linda Darnell in final scene
p. 89: Billy Ward and Linda Darnell in final scene

The Flame of New Orleans (1941, directed by René Clair)
pp. 90/91: Marlene Dietrich in opera-house sequence, design and film frames

Centennial Summer (1946, directed by Otto Preminger)
p. 92: "Julia, Change 1, Street Outfit, 1876," design for Jeanne Crain
p. 93: "Linda Darnell as Edith," scenes 42–47 and 52–53, screen test

Désirée (1954, directed by Henry Koster)
pp. 94/95: design for Jean Simmons and screen test

volants de tulle
application
or
tulle noir
pantalon
turque
tissus
fulgurant
transparent
tulle
très

Wilson
Change?
René Hubert
1944
Hallway Tea – meeting Wilson
Spring 1915

10 yds Brocade
Size 36
504-49

Julia
change I.
PART OF: JULIA ROGERS
PLAYED BY:
CHANGE #1 Street outfit 1876
WORN:
EXT. OFFICIALS' PLATFORM
CENTENNIAL EXPOSITION - Day
Scenes 2-3
EXT. STREET & ROGERS' HOUSE
Scene 4
INT. FOYER
Scene 5
INT. PARLOR - Nite
Scenes 6 - 8 - 10
The Rogers family listening to the President's speech -- Rogers is annoyed because he can't hear what is being said -- they return home and make preparations for dinner -- company calls and Edith entertains Ben on the porch.
479 7-31-45
OP
Jean Crain 47914- Ethel

PREMINGER – A 479
LINDA DARNELL
AS "EDITH"
Ch #5A
INT. FOYER – 42
EXT-STREET – 42-43
EXT- EXPOSITION. 44
EXT-CENTENNIAL STREET 45
EXT-FRENCH BLDG. 46-47
INT. FRENCH PAVILION 48-52
INT. CLOCK-EXHIBIT 53
9/4/45 DESIGNER – HUBERT

"Hubert's designs, whether for contemporary or period costumes, are generally striking in their graphic quality.... In scale, pattern and texture, these costumes are emphatically designed for the big screen."

Amy Sargeant

Time Traveling across the Channel: Hubert, Korda and London Films

Amy Sargeant

In his preface to the catalog accompanying the 2002 exhibition *Les plus belles robes du cinéma,* the then president of the Cinémathèque Française asked why only historical films are called "costume films" and why such films routinely receive awards for costume design – Oscars or Césars.[1] Filmographies, including that of René Hubert, acknowledge films set in the past alongside films with a contemporary setting. Some credited designers were established couturiers, appointed to produce wardrobes for particular stars or films – from Poiret and Lanvin in the silent period to, more recently, Cardin, Saint Laurent, Lagerfeld and Lacroix. Some items in the Cinémathèque collection remain unattributed to a film or designer, even when they are known to have been created for and worn by a specific star. Yet more recently the contribution of generic costume suppliers has been credited by way of BAFTA's recognition in 2016 of the London costumer and rental firm Angels.

While working for London Films from 1935 until 1940, Hubert designed and supervised costumes for both historical films (*Fire over England,* 1937, and *That Hamilton Woman,* 1941) and films with a contemporary setting (*The Divorce of Lady X,* 1938). In the same way as with many costume films there is generally a blurring and compromise between historical authenticity and an appeal to the tastes of a modern audience. Additionally, I am also struck by the number of films for which Hubert provided historical or contemporary costumes set against, by way of contrast, fancy dress events: Merle Oberon's tiered and ribboned crinoline confection in *The Divorce of Lady* X, *The Ghost Goes West*'s ocean liner entertainment and *That Hamilton Woman*'s turn-of-the-century ball.

Hubert was one of a number of foreign personnel appointed by the producer Alexander Korda's London Films titles for their perceived technical prowess. These included the French directors René Clair (*The*

Robert Donat and Marlene Dietrich in *Knight Without Armour* (1937)

Ghost Goes West, 1935) and Jacques Feyder (*Knight Without Armour,* 1937). The émigré Russian designers Andrei Andreiev (*Dark Journey,* 1937) and Lazare Meerson (*Fire over England* and *Knight Without Armour*) were likewise employed. Korda's brother Vincent designed sets for *That Hamilton Woman* and *Things to Come* (1936), while his brother Zoltan directed *The Four Feathers* (1939) with Hubert, again, supervising costumes. The Korda brothers' fellow Hungarian Miklós Rózsa supplied scoring for several films. Arthur Wimperis and the Hungarian Lajos Biró were frequent collaborators on scripts and dialogue.

Korda's biographer Paul Tabori sometimes teased his English friends by saying that "the paragon of Englishmen" in *The Scarlet Pimpernel* (1934) was the creation of *three* Hungarians: Baroness Orczy, daughter of an Hungarian aristocrat; Korda; and Leslie Howard (born Leslie Stainer), who came to England in his early teens.[2] Oberon, who appeared alongside Howard in *The Scarlet Pimpernel,* subsequently married Korda. Such appointments promoted the international marketability of London Films, offsetting their high – when not actually ruinous – costs of production.

Robert Donat, star of *The Ghost Goes West* and *Knight Without Armour,* commented about Korda: "I think of him as three personalities. The Dreamer, planning wonders that could never happen, only in the never-never land. The Practical – yet invariably biting off twenty-two times one hundred percent more than he can chew. The Worldbeater."[3] Hubert's costume designs frequently featured in trade and press publicity as an attractive marketing asset, promoting Korda's extensive ambitions.

Vivien Leigh in *Fire over England* (1937)

Disguises, Decoys and Alibis

Hubert contributed to the collective effort to deliver *Knight Without Armour* as a star vehicle for Marlene Dietrich and to reinforce her star image, having previously known her in Berlin. Wimperis and Biró produced dialogue that drew audience attention to Dietrich as Dietrich. When Fothergill (Donat) advises Countess Alexandra (Dietrich) to dress less conspicuously, for her own safety on her escorted journey to Petrograd, she adopts peasant garb. However, the shawl tied around her face emphatically defines the already recognizable, conspicuously composed Dietrich oval mask: finely penciled eyebrows, heavily lashed eyelids, the shaded nose, highlighted cheekbones and glossed lips – a look already systematically established for her by Josef von Sternberg in, not least, *The Scarlet Empress* (1934).

The film opens at Ascot in 1913 – both an event in the social calendar and an occasion for sartorial display, most famously by way of statement hats.[4] An overhead shot shows a gaggle of gray top-hatted punters, men in tailored morning dress abiding by a strictly imposed code. Blonde Dietrich is introduced – revealed – center of frame as she turns her head directly toward the camera in response to a greeting, simultaneously establishing her position as the star and the social status of her character. The brim of her wheel hat dips to cast a shadow over her right eye, its layers of net echoing the airy upper sleeves of her suitably pale summery frock.[5] But Alexandra and her father are not staying for the remainder of the season: there is plenty of shooting to be had at home, he remarks portentously. Elsewhere on the track a conventionally bowler-hatted Fothergill makes a small patriotic bet on the king's horse.

While Alexandra is presented at court, Fothergill, adopting the alias Uranov, is dispatched to infiltrate a revolutionary cell and is duly sent to Siberia. Emerging as a leather-jacketed and peak-capped hero of the proletariat, Fothergill is cast on the opposite side of the revolution. He first knowingly encounters her in 1917, framed by a mirror, echoing the St. Petersburg mirrors by which she was surrounded on the eve of her wedding.

Escaping arrest in a forest, Alexandra dons an army greatcoat and shaggy fur hat, matching Uranov. But the face remains consistently, unambiguously the same. When the countess finds herself in safe company among White Russians, she requests a bath, and a maid taunts her admirers (as much in the film's audience as in the film) with the comment "You don't know what you're missing." A mountain of gowns are thrust into the eager arms of the servant for a choice to be made for Alexandra's grand entry to the assembly of dinner guests. Dietrich appears in a sleek, dark, sequined sheath dress, accentuating the full length of her body (as famous for its legs as its face), again familiar from Dietrich appearances on screen and off. A series of staircases marks Alexandra's arrival to maximum effect. Little wonder that Donat, who had himself obtained the rights to James Hilton's source novel, was irked to find himself upstaged.[6]

Meerson's sets showcase Dietrich, sometimes by way of a unified visual theme. At home at her country residence, the countess awakes to a silence broken only by clock chimes and the multiple bells she rings to summon her servants. The calls go unanswered. A morning breeze wafts the curtains of her sumptuously pale and padded bedroom, echoing the billowing drapery of her gown as she dashes through the palace to discover the servants' revolt. A length of the light chiffon veiling is torn and seized as a mocking trophy of aristocratic luxury, prior to the ransacking and destruction of the estate. Alexandra's person is as much under threat as her property.

Whereas Dietrich was already an established star in 1937, Vivien Leigh was being groomed by Korda for stardom. In *Dark Journey* the variety of Hubert's costumes serve as an advertisement for her character's business: Madeleine Goddard runs an elite fashion boutique in Stockholm. Superficially, Madeleine, using a Swiss identity, appears impartial, insisting to her assistants that she does not "want French women nor German women. I just want saleswomen." But, as it transpires, her frequent trips since 1915 between neutral Sweden and war-torn France are for reasons other than professional. Patterns ingeniously embroidered onto the sheer fabric of glamorous Parisian evening gowns, "the latest French designs," reveal military positions when placed over lampshades. Madeleine delivers information to German agents and is duly rewarded: she is termed "a very expensive luxury."

Opening in the spring of 1918, *Dark Journey* foreshadows the European war to come, its impact amplified by the contemporaneity of the costumes: slim bias-cut waisted and sometimes peplumed calf-length dresses, extended shoulders. When not in cowled leopard print with matching accessories, Leigh is often dressed in starkly contrasting matte dark robes with white detailing (a familiar Hubert/Leigh motif), collars or ruffles framing a heart-shaped neckline. Leigh is here coupled with the émigré actor Conrad Veidt as the nonchalantly debonair playboy German baron Karl von Marwitz, who is living in self-imposed luxurious exile. He arrives immaculately suited with a camel coat worn casually over his shoulders and has ample funds to dispense at Madeleine's boutique on presents to be gifted to loose women. Neither Madeleine nor Karl are quite what they seem. For Karl, wardrobe serves as a decoy; for Madeleine, wardrobe is an alibi. In 1937 it was not entirely clear in what capacity Madeleine intended her farewell to a finally service-uniformed and more severe, less frivolous Karl: but she'll see him again, she says.

Conrad Veidt and Vivien Leigh in *Dark Journey* (1937)

Period Costume and Contemporary Propaganda: Looking Back

After the transatlantic success of *The Private Life of Henry VIII* (1933), London Films attempted to repeat the formula in 1934 with *Catherine the Great* (casting Flora Robson as the older empress) and *The Private Life of Don Juan*. The *Spectator* critic, Charles Davy, noted that Korda was cornering the personal history of European monarchs.[7] Sue Harper has suggested that *Fire over England* (supported by the Ministry of Information), with Robson as Elizabeth I, was not critically well received and that its pro-rearmament views were not politically popular in 1937. Furthermore, its love interest was weak: "Korda preferred historical figures who could attain mythological status and who could tap a range of audience feelings about national identity, class composition, and sexual pleasure."[8]

Korda told Laurence Olivier that propaganda can be a bitter medicine requiring sugar coating, "and *Lady Hamilton* is a very thick sugar coating indeed."[9] Korda was keen to emphasize the private "bedroom aspect" alongside Nelson's public career. *That Hamilton Woman* (supported by the Foreign Office) duly proved enormously popular, not least by way of its casting of Olivier and Leigh, who had provided tepid love interest in *Fire over England* but who had embarked upon a much publicized and tempestuous off-screen affair during the course of filming. Publicity for *That Hamilton Woman* vaunted Olivier and Leigh as "the World's most Glamorous Couple," comparing Emma to Cleopatra and Helen of Troy.[10]

Olivier had appeared opposite Oberon and with Robson in William Wyler's 1939 *Wuthering Heights*; Leigh's star status had been confirmed by her billing in David O. Selznick's 1939 *Gone With the Wind*, the biggest box-office picture in the industry to date. The "timely" political message of *That Hamilton Woman*, likewise shot in Hollywood, is unambiguous, with Nelson (Olivier) warning of the threat of invasion after the Battle of Copenhagen (1801): "You cannot make peace with dictators." The success of the film was further enhanced by Winston Churchill's personal endorsement – reportedly his favorite picture and viewed repeatedly. Perhaps he cared to associate himself with Nelson – "There's no one else" – and was certainly keen to retain a hold on Empire. Elizabeth's stylized military frogging in *Fire over England* is matched by Emma's patriotically naval outfit in *That Hamilton Woman*.

Exhibitors were encouraged to use Hubert's forty-two items of costuming for Leigh as an advertisement, most obviously attracting a female clientele

Design for Vivien Leigh in *That Hamilton Woman* (1941)

presumed to constitute the majority of cinema audiences.[11] Keith Lodwick suggests that designs for the film had a major impact on early 1940s fashion: "On offer is an evening cape, like the one Lady Hamilton wore on board Nelson's ship; Regency frills, double collars and fichu-dresses will all be back in vogue."[12] A pressbook meanwhile singled out for special mention an outfit worn for a gala opera performance: "A Gainsborough hat of pink velvet trimmed in oversize ostrich plumes."[13] Reputedly, Leigh issued conditions for her millinery in *Gone With the Wind*: "All I ask is – don't let them see the hat before they see my face."[14] In *That Hamilton Woman* a dark hat and dark hair graphically announce an indistinct Leigh, appearing as background to the film's title sequence. The action is then located with Emma, once renowned as "the most beautiful woman in the world," now destitute in Calais, before reminiscing to an appreciative audience (her companion in jail) about her own glorious ascent from prostitution prior to her ignominious fall: "Go on, tell us all about it – doesn't matter if it's true or not." It's the story that matters.

Hubert's costumes for *That Hamilton Woman* serve several agendas simultaneously. First, they convey the chronology of the narrative from Emma's introduction at age eighteen to Lord Hamilton in Naples, through her longstanding affair with Nelson, then her receiving news after Nelson's death at Trafalgar in 1805 and the disregarding, subsequently, of Nelson's "bequest to the nation." Socially, Emma's costuming records, retrospectively, Emma's rise (her engagements with various minor European kingdoms) and demise (her London lodgings), then English rural retreat marked by mutton-sleeved dresses in small floral-pattern cotton prints. Then, her punishing return to a gutter.

At Emma's second meeting with Nelson she is shocked to see his previously impressive vigor already diminished, his right eye closed and his sleeve pinned to his chest. Yet Nelson matches his battle scars and wounds with an accumulation of medals awarded for bravery and decorations marking his rise through the ranks of the navy and his elevation through the peerage. Indeed, Nelson's vanity, his determination to wear in battle the medals won in battle, eventually proves his downfall. Hatbands indicate various ships under Nelson's command at the Battle of Trafalgar as sailors read his momentous flag signal: "England Expects That Every Man Will Do His Duty."

That Hamilton Woman (1941)

Design for Vivien Leigh

Vivien Leigh and Laurence Olivier

While "historic" engravings are used to authenticate locations, Emma's introduction is accompanied by a painting of Leigh posed in the manner of George Romney, whose portraits (and prints thereof, distributed for popular consumption, akin to fan photos of Leigh) had served to establish Emma's celebrity in the 1780s.[15] Hubert's costumes draw on portraits as models for imitation, the film vaunts its source material, and Lord Hamilton, as antiquarian and connoisseur, comments on Emma as an object whom he seeks to add to his collection of exquisite artifacts.

Second, Hubert's outfits serve to distinguish her from Lady Nelson, as much as the object of scurrilous caricatures in her lifetime were an increasingly plump Emma and the notoriously diminutive, besotted Nelson.[16] Emma's vivacity and sensuality are set against Lady Nelson's tight-lipped dourness and respect for social propriety: she breakfasts on tea with lemon and thinly buttered toast. Lady Nelson makes her first appearance in a dull, flatly woven plain gown worn over a tightly collared shirt with multiple small buttons and a brooch at her throat. She is thoroughly buttoned up, weedy and in mourning dress. Her bonnets fail to attract attention to herself or themselves. However, even Lady Nelson dresses for dinner and thus wears satin – albeit drab. Emma models the paler, more youthful "Grecian" style she has herself hitherto popularized, its loose folds, it transpires, possibly disguising pregnancy – her fainting "natural to women of all classes" – subsequently remarked on by gossips at the House of Lords gallery.

Hubert's extravagant costumes, award-nominated cinematography, set design, special effects and award-winning sound magnificently combine and contrive in the millennial ball episode to convey Emma's engulfing passion. Not for the first time, Emma traverses the vast expanse of the embassy and flings open the wondrously glazed doors to the balcony, with a trompe l'oeil view of the sea and the fleet beyond augmenting the depth of the scene >pp. 109–17. In honor of her lover Emma wears a parure of initialed diamanté pendant and earrings. In homage to the century just passing (it spans, Nelson reminds us, from Marlborough to Peter the Great to Bonaparte; "and Nelson," adds Emma), Leigh wears a heavily encrusted gown with a voluminous paniered skirt over a padded underskirt, her neat waist accentuated. Scale, contrast and patterning ensure that her figure occupies considerable space in the frame as she sweeps to the balcony.

Whereas Leigh, as Scarlett O'Hara in *Gone With the Wind,* famously wore a velvet gown improvised and tailored from curtains and passementerie, Leigh,

***That Hamilton Woman* (1941)**

Vivien Leigh

Costumes for Laurence Olivier and Vivien Leigh, in exhibition *René Hubert – Kleider machen Stars*, Museum für Gestaltung Zürich, 2021, photograph by Museum für Gestaltung Zürich

as Emma, is perhaps more upholstered than dressed. But, it seems to me, Hubert's design here achieves more than spectacular display and speaks to additional purpose. The anachronistic asymmetry of Emma's ruched bodice graphically echoes the diagonal of Nelson's ceremonial sash and the tones and textures of his uniform, again reiterating an ideal romantic coupling. Pam Cook observes that costume drama's masquerade "is a prime vehicle for the exploration of identity, encouraging cross-dressing, not only between characters but metaphorically between characters and spectators in the sense that the latter can be seen as trying on a variety of roles."[17] Leigh's costume changes in *That Hamilton Woman* serve as more than an attraction; they provide the occasion for emotional investment on the part of the audience with the waxing and waning of Emma's fortunes.

Contemporary Propaganda: Looking Forward

For *Things to Come,* Hubert shared costume credits with John Armstrong (with whom he had previously worked on *The Ghost Goes West*) and the Marchioness of Queensberry. Or, one might say, he further shared with H. G. Wells. Wells secured a guarantee from Korda, in collaboration with the director William Cameron Menzies (a former production designer himself), that he would supervise all aspects of the screen adaptation of his 1933 "spree" *The Shape of Things to Come: The Ultimate Revolution.*[18] If *Fire over England* and *That Hamilton Woman* were overtly intended as contemporary propaganda by way of the past, *Things to Come* proselytized for a particular Wellesian view of the future, as a paean to his faith in socialism, internationalism and scientific progress.

His presence on set frequently proved overbearing and, as Christopher Frayling comments, "In his dealings with Korda's team he was generally better at saying what he *didn't* want than at clarifying what he *did.*"[19] This may well account for the absence in the film of Hubert's various proposals for translucent wire-edged millinery. Feminine frivolity in 2036 is discretely restricted to Rowena (Margaretta Scott). "A higher phase of civilization" is marked as much by the design of clothing as by architecture, gadgetry and modes of transport.

In the 1960s, following years of war and pestilence, the country has descended to brigandage and subjects dress themselves, as best they can, in foraged rags. Wells suggested a "sluttish magnificence"

Costume with hat for *Things to Come* (1936)

Flora Robson, Vivien Leigh and Morton Selten in *Fire over England* (1937)

for the barbaric Roxana (Margaretta Scott). Roxana's consort, the Boss (Ralph Richardson), wears sheepskin over his black uniform, and a rosette on his helmet connotes a Tudor rose and a debased patriotism. Richardson described his ensemble as an amalgam of Boy Scout, Far West cowboy and Cossack.[20] However, Mussolini, explicitly cited in Wells' 1933 political critique, was not convinced by any disclaimer that the Boss was not intended as a caricature, and *Things to Come* was banned in Fascist Italy.[21] Recognizably contemporary features of dress are again used, here to provide deliberate dystopian commentary and effect.

Costuming in the utopia of 2036 is spartan and androgynous, conveying Wells' vision of more egalitarian pairings. Both men and women wear short hygienic white togas with sandals, Wells predicting that people of the future would be fitter and healthier (and everything "lovelier")[22] >pp. 118-21. While Vincent Korda exploited a new display plastic, rhodoid, for decluttered and imposing futuristic sets, the wide yokes of the costumes were padded with hard foam to produce an equally stunning outline. The progress of technology allows for extruded and molded materials (inconspicuous labor) as opposed to the farming, skinning, weaving and knitting of primary natural resources.

A child (in a miniature version of the uniform toga) disingenuously questions the wisdom of American skyscrapers – in 2036 considered archaic, she is informed: the present is delivered as a history lesson. One reviewer, remarking on the film's unisex miniskirts, meanwhile identified the padded yokes as samurai inspired.[23] Wells' instructions prompted "fine clothes [...] more utilitarian than decorative" (the yokes were to incorporate gadgetry).[24] By way of contrast, the incurable romantic and reactionary artist Theotocopulos (Cedric Hardwicke) wears buckled shoes of an *ancien régime* and a flamboyant cloak. Emblematically, he resists revolution and scientific progress.

In conclusion, Hubert's designs, whether for contemporary or period costumes, are generally striking in their graphic quality. This is exemplified by the cut of Oberon's necklines in *The Divorce of Lady X,* Donat's plaid (rather than authentic tartan) in *The Ghost Goes West,* the bold geometric appliqué on farthingales in *Fire over England,* the curvilinear embossed panniers of Leigh's ballgown in *That Hamilton Woman* and the toga yokes of *Things to Come.* In scale, pattern and texture, these costumes are emphatically designed for the big screen.

1 Jean Charles Tacchella, "Tout ce que les costumes peuvent ajouter à un film...," *Les Plus Belles robes du cinéma,* Paris, 2001, p. 12.
2 Paul Tabori, *Alexander Korda,* London, 1959, p. 22.
3 Donat in *The Picturegoer*, cited in Amy Sargeant, *British Cinema: A Critical History,* London, 2005, p. 124.
4 In *My Fair Lady* (George Cukor, 1964), with Audrey Hepburn costumed and hatted by Cecil Beaton, acceptance at Ascot suitably marks the apotheosis of Eliza Doolittle.
5 For a comparable 1934 butterfly sleeve dress, see James Laver, *A Concise History of Costume,* London, 1969, p. 152.
6 Sargeant, *British Cinema,* p. 126.
7 Charles Davy review, *The Spectator,* February 2, 1934, p. 235.
8 Sue Harper, *Picturing the Past: The Rise and Fall of the British Costume Film,* London, 1994, p. 91.
9 Quoted in Charles Drazin, *Alexander Korda: Britain's Only Movie Mogul,* London, 2002, p. 236.
10 BFI Special Materials, Exhibitors' Campaign Book, *That Hamilton Woman,* p. 3.
11 Ibid., p. 6.
12 V&A Vivien Leigh Archive, cited in Keith Lodwick, "Dressing the Part: Costume and Character," in *Vivien Leigh: Actress and Icon,* ed. Kate Dorney and Maggie B. Gale, Manchester, 2018, p. 176.
13 Exhibitors' Campaign Book, p. 7.
14 Drake Stutesman, "Storytelling: Marlene Dietrich's Face and John Frederics' Hats," in *Fashioning Film Stars,* ed. Rachel Moseley, London, 2005, p. 30.
15 See Tim Clayton, "Figures of Fame," in *Joshua Reynolds: The Creation of Celebrity,* ed. Martin Postle, London, 2005, p. 55.
16 See Amy Sargeant, "Do we need another hero?" in *British Historical Cinema,* ed. Claire Monk and Amy Sargeant, London, 2002, pp. 23–24.
17 Pam Cook, *Fashioning the Nation: Costume and Identity in British Cinema,* London, 1996, p. 6.
18 Christopher Frayling, *Things to Come,* London, 1995, p. 6.
19 Ibid., p. 50.
20 Ibid., p. 25.
21 H. G. Wells, *The Shape of Things to Come* (London: Hutchinson, 1933), p. 193; Frayling, ibid., p. 26.
22 H. G. Wells, *Things to Come,* London, 1935, p. 95.
23 Alistair Cooke, cited in Frayling, *Things to Come,* p. 71.
24 Wells, *Things to Come,* pp. 14 and 16.

Look Back and Look Ahead

That Hamilton Woman (1941, directed by Alexander Korda)
p. 109: design for Vivien Leigh
pp. 110–115: from salon to balcony in Naples, film frames
pp. 116/117: Vivien Leigh and Laurence Olivier on balcony in Naples

Things to Come (1936, directed by William Cameron Menzies):
pp. 118/119: Kenneth Villiers and Raymond Massey
p. 120: underground city of the future
p. 121: Sophie Stewart and Pearl Argyle

A.K_55600-48

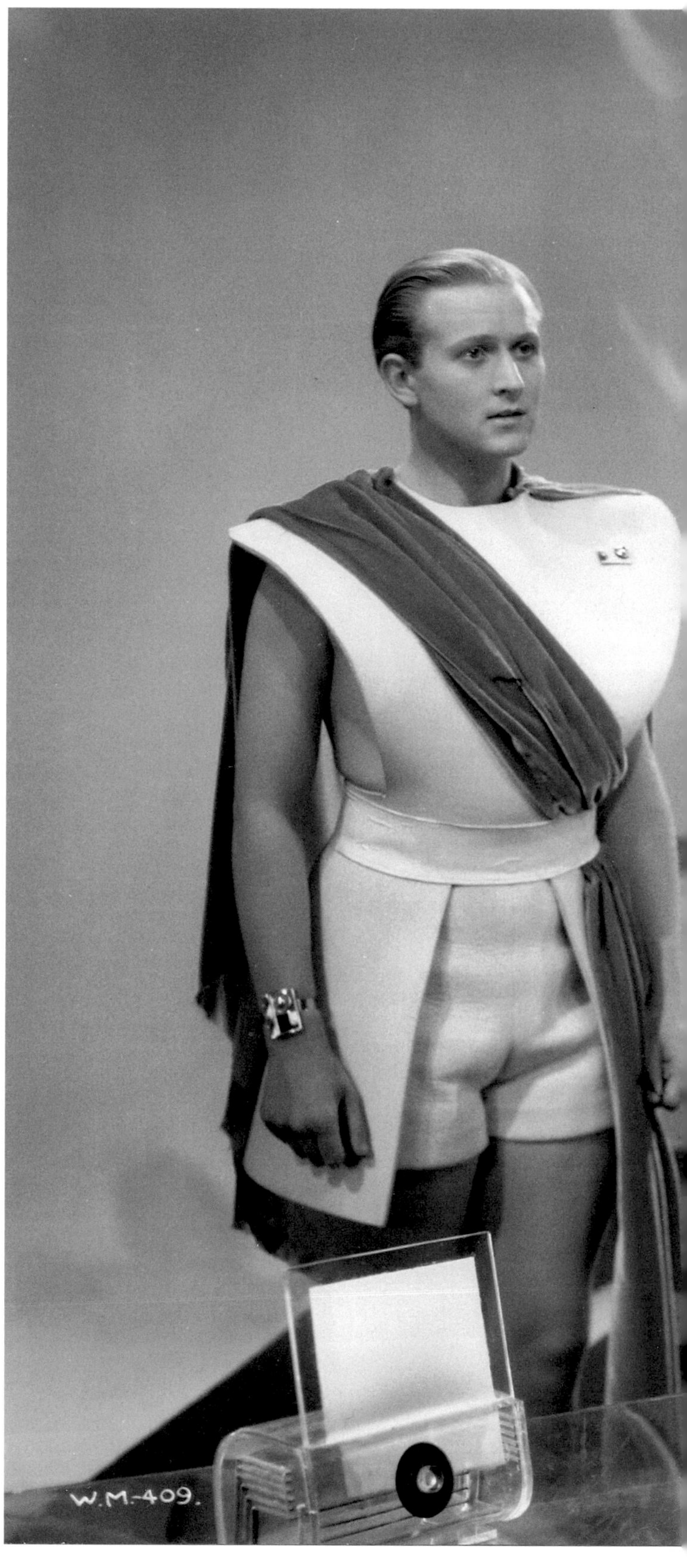
W.M.-409.

W.M. 510.

W.M. 438

“Photographs from Hubert’s early years in Hollywood already reveal a great deal of self-confidence. Rather than with a needle and thread, he is portrayed with a brush and palette in reference to his training at the Académie des Beaux-Arts in Paris.”

Roland Fischer-Briand

Photographs from the Studio: On Costume Photography as a Work and Marketing Tool

Roland Fischer-Briand

In contrast to the moving images in its "younger brother" film, the static medium of photography involves a decisive advantage: it can be perceived apart from ephemeral cinema projections. The spectrum of possible uses in the context of a film production ranges from advertising to tools employed in the industry and reproduction of other media, such as designs.[1]

René Hubert left behind several hundred prints of his photographs – including photographs of or for stage productions, fashion shots and photos from his private life. The vast majority, film stills, cover all five decades of his work on both sides of the Atlantic. In this contribution they serve as a starting point for an examination of the characteristics of this special genre of photographs when used for advertising purposes.

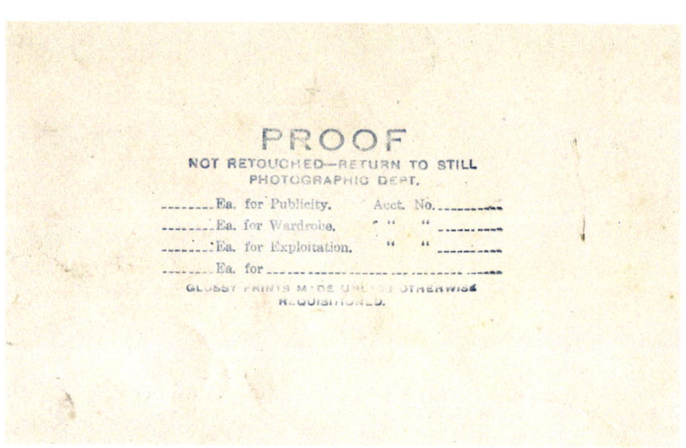

Reverse of a film still from *Quality Street* (1927, Metro-Goldwyn-Mayer)

Top and center right: Gloria Swanson in *Father Takes a Wife* (1941), photograph by Ernest A. Bachrach

Bottom right: Gloria Swanson in *The Love of Sunya* (1927), photograph by Russell Ball

> "Le roman d'une robe cinema" ("The Story of a Film Costume"), double page from *Cinémonde*, no. 196 (1932)

Put in the Proper Light

Studio portraits taken off film sets were the pinnacle of the work of studios' photography departments and the domain of their chief photographers. Portraits represent an exception because their creators were not kept secret, unlike the work of on-set photographers.[2] A who's who of studio photographers working in Hollywood who influenced the decades of glamour can be found in Hubert's collection, including the work of Clarence S. Bull (MGM), Ruth Harriet Louise (MGM), George Hurrell (MGM, Warner Bros., Columbia), Ernest A. Bachrach (RKO) and George Platt Lynes (Vogue Hollywood).

These names were associated with the star systems of the major film studios, which the Swiss costume designer was an integral part of: in the course of his career Hubert was under contract at numerous Hollywood studios, where he was one of a dozen renowned couturiers who created costumes, such as Adrian, Travis Banton, Howard Greer, Edith Head and Irene. These chief costume designers dressed the stars, while the studio's own fashion costume department took care of most supporting actors and extras.

In the case of portraits the staging of film costumes in photographs resulted in a sort of competition that was difficult to resolve, which alternated between the visual appeal of luxurious clothes and the star's attraction. This is especially true for historical dramas and film spectacles, which were Hubert's specialty. Depending on the genre, unique visual conventions for film stills were developed that can be perceived in his work.

While moving images are able to demonstrate the advantages and various facets of a design in a temporal sequence, using other means was required in the static medium of photography. For example, positioning the subject on a staircase or pedestal was effective for creating sufficient space for sweeping gowns and trains. Recamiers or formally reduced blocks were appealing for a number of lying or half-sitting positions and provided a setting for draping opulently flowing dresses, thereby presenting them to the greatest advantage. The images also suggest the star's (ambivalent) availability, as erotic staging of the female body, its cleavage and therefore sex appeal was a proven method of enticing members of the public to purchase tickets. Hubert's fashion was also suitable for this purpose. The "Hubert slit" in dresses, which was named after him, helped photographers present the subject's legs suggestively.

Cleverly positioned side lighting was employed to dramatically accentuate the arrangement of folds. Drastically dimmed lighting made the reflections of sequins or rhinestones shine in an impressive way. Accessories such as handbags, fans or hats could provide a pretext to hold arms away from the body and highlight contours. Photographers also used props that were not necessarily in the film, such as a column that the actor leaned against, which provided a clear view of her silhouette and therefore the costume. Taken in front of a white background and therefore visually removed from the film's setting, these photographs created an imaginary hybrid space that alternates between the character and the real-life person. Furthermore, this optical dissociation provided the practical advantage of being suitable for additional publicity purposes.

While in traditional performance photographs, looking directly at the camera and therefore the viewer was still not permitted so as to avoid destroying the illusion of the film, eye contact was welcome in portrait photography. But occasionally the stars'

LE
D'UN
DE

MADAME, m'écrit une lectrice, qui a sans doute constaté avec désespoir l'insuffisance de sa garde-robe, ne pourriez-vous me dire ce que deviennent les toilettes portées à l'écran par les artistes ? »

C'est une question que bien des femmes se sont déjà posée. Quelques-unes, plus hardies, ont été jusqu'à écrire à des vedettes en leur exposant leur gêne momentanée, et en les priant de leur envoyer une des robes de leur dernier film pour aller à leur premier bal ou au mariage de leur cousine.

Je vais donc vous parler aujourd'hui de la robe de cinéma. Lorsque j'étais écolière, j'ai eu successivement à traiter, selon l'imagination débordante de mes professeurs, les sujets suivants : histoire d'un sou... ou d'un cheval de course... ou d'une barre de fer, et j'y démontrais abondamment, comme le voulait la tradition, que le sou, le cheval ou la poutre, après avoir été beau comme un sou neuf, dorlotté comme un pur sang et forgé avec fierté, s'étaient vus dégringoler l'échelle des honneurs pour finir dans le fond d'un tronc d'église, entre les brancards d'un fiacre et à la foire à la ferraille. Ce qui permet de tirer une moralité âpre et peu rassurante sur ce qui nous attend lorsque nous serons vieux.

Les robes de cinéma suivent, elles aussi, cette courbe d'existence, et je vais recommencer, pour vous, la rédaction de mes joyeuses années scolaires...

... Cette histoire commence aux studios Paramount.

J'ai déjà comparé ceux-ci à une noix verte, celle-là même sur laquelle rechignait la guenon de la fable. Il faut en effet traverser l'écorce amère que j'appellerais les « remparts » de ce studio-forteresse avant d'arriver jusqu'à l'amande, c'est-à-dire à un groupe de personnalités éminentes et charmantes, et entre autres à René Hubert...

René Hubert habite dans un grand studio clair et briliant comme une salle de conte de fées : blanc, argent, acier et miroir... Il est assis devant une grande table et manie des fusains et des pinceaux... Ou bien, dans les cabines d'essayage, il drape des satins et des plumes sur les plus jolies filles de la terre...

René Hubert est souriant, courtois, aimable et heureux de son sort. Ses secrétaires et ses employés, et les artistes l'adorent et n'en disent que du bien, même lorsqu'il n'est pas là, et ceci, dans le monde du cinéma comme dans tous les autres, est si inattendu que ce seul fait le signalerait à notre attention. René Hubert est le Pétrone du studio.

Dès qu'une artiste est engagée par Paramount, elle est conduite chez le photographe et chez Hubert. Il lui offre un fauteuil, bavarde quelques instants avec elle, et pendant ce temps son regard précis la détaille, note au passage tel petit défaut et tel avantage physique, l'un qu'il faudra dissimuler, l'autre qu'il faudra mettre en valeur.

Puis, après avoir étudié le scénario du film, il commence ces maquettes qui sont chacune un petit chef-d'œuvre d'élégance et d'esprit.

A Hollywood d'abord (où pendant de longues années, il fut l'exclusif modelliste de Gloria Swanson), à Berlin ensuite où il habilla avec tant de fantaisie groupe de personnalités éminentes et charmantes et le délicieux : « Chemin du Paradis », il a appris les grandes lois de l'élégance cinématographique, qui se dégage de l'harmonie d'un ensemble plus que de la perfection d'un détail.

Il connait les tissus photogéniques, sait éviter le chatoiement flatteur mais dangereux d'un satin, la lourdeur d'un drapé, l'ombre gênante d'un chapeau sur un visage.

Il sait surtout diversifier à l'infini ses modèles non seulement d'après la femme qu'il habille, mais aussi d'après le personnage qu'elle incarne dans un film.

Pour une jeune fille mince, moderne, délurée, étudiante pas très riche, il compose des tailleurs nets et simples, égayés d'un col blanc, d'une cravate amusante : ceux de Meg Lemonnier dans *Il est charmant.*

Pour une belle Anglaise oisive, coquette, il compose au contraire des toilettes très féminines, allie le velours noir aux larges broderies perlées : celles de Betty Stockfield dans *Une Nuit à l'Hôtel.*

Il enveloppe les opérettes dans l'organdi et la mousseline, y fait palpiter l'envol des capelines de crin clair, pare les vamps de robes moulantes, audacieusement ouvertes aux aisselles, au creux du dos, en coins de chair affolants...

La robe, pour lui, est un état d'âme. Il en est le magicien. Sa devise pourrait être : « Dis-moi comment tu t'habilles, je te dirai qui tu es... »

Devise sage. Une femme nue est pour qui réfléchit,

René Hubert... On remarque derr

De haut en bas :
Quelques modèles de René Hubert pour Edwige Feuillère, Gloria Swanson, Danièle Brégis, Jackie Monnier.

592

MAN
ROBE
NÉMA

terriblement déroutante et mystérieuse. Son corps lisse ne livre rien de son âme ; alors qu'elle peut démasquer sa vanité par une broche trop voyante, sa frivolité par un volant trop fragile, sa loyauté par la ligne sûre d'un tailleur.

Et c'est pourquoi, en marge des dessins de travail d'Hubert on peut lire ces annotations déconcertantes :

« Une femme qui parle fort. »

« Une petite jeune fille rougissante. »

« Une femme mariée ayant des chagrins d'amour... »

Lorsque Hubert se lève et fait un geste, ses collaboratrices accourent, des robes pleins les bras. Il en pleut sur le grand sofa gris, sur le dossier des chaises, et les rondes boîtes à chapeaux s'étagent en pyramides instables. Hubert caresse de la main les tissus soyeux et rêches comme s'il allait leur donner de la vie. Il les connaît tous, et dans chaque détail. Il se souvient de la pince à faire à la taille de cette romantique robe de mousseline rose, et des boutons de cristal de cette veste de golf. Les accessoires entourent la robe, en troupeau charmé et charmant ; c'est le bibi adorable, le manchon de fleurs, les gants travaillés de découpes, le collier original, l'écharpe et le petit sac... René Hubert est aussi prophète... Il habille les films qu'on tournera demain, qu'on verra après-demain, à la mode de la saison prochaine, qu'il lancera... Il a des merveilles plein ses placards. Il en a plus encore dans ses pinceaux, ses pots de gouache et d'encre de Chine, dans ses mains fines et déliées, aux beaux ongles soignés.

Et derrière le beau studio de miroir et d'argent, il y a les ateliers où l'on taille, assemble et bâtit, et où l'aiguille court plus souvent dans la soie que dans la laine...

La robe est achevée, essayée, approuvée par le patron à qui rien n'échappe. La vedette l'a portée au studio pendant deux jours. On la verra à l'écran pendant cinq minutes... La vie de la robe merveilleuse est-elle achevée ?

Evidemment non... Cela représenterait une dépense trop colossale. Car les robes de René Hubert ne sont pas faites de tarlatane, de soie artificielle, de paillettes, de toile à cataplasme et de papier gauffré comme les travestis du Mardi-Gras ou les costumes de scène des petits cirques de province. Les tissus bon marché n'ont ni la souplesse, ni le moelleux, ni le poids, ni le reflet qu'exigent les robes de cinéma. Il n'est donc employé que des tissus de première qualité, et il n'est pas rare que des toilettes de vedettes reviennent aussi cher qu'une robe de grande maison.

Une robe n'est donc pas mise en retraite après avoir été portée par celle pour qui elle a été faite. Il arrive que l'artiste, séduite par sa forme ou sa couleur, décide de la conserver pour la ville et l'achète au studio. Ce fut le cas pour le fameux pyjama de soie noire de Fernand Gravey dans *Tu seras duchesse*. Mais c'est assez rare, les couleurs employées pour l'écran étant difficilement portables à la ville. On sait en effet que les chemises des hommes, les robes de mariées, et tout ce qui apparaît blanc est en réalité bleu. L'utilisation exacte des nuances qui s'harmonisent à l'écran oblige parfois à des assemblages de tons assez curieux. Aussi les robes restent souvent au studio, où elles sont confiées à des habilleuses qui veillent à ne pas les laisser se faner. Retouchées, un peu modifiées, elles habilleront des rôles secondaires, puis des figurantes.

Puis, périodiquement, lorsqu'elles sont devenues trop nombreuses (il y a parfois plus de deux mille modèles différents suspendus aux cintres des magasins d'habillement), René Hubert organise, pour les employées et ouvrières du studio, une vente. Les robes y sont cédées pour cent ou cent cinquante francs, offrant ainsi aux jeunes filles de Paramount la robe de soirée chic qu'elles n'auraient jamais pu espérer. Cinquante francs de nettoyage, un petit relâchage des coutures (elles sont si minces, ces vedettes) et voilà, pour le prix d'une petite robe de confection, une toilette complète, créée par un des maîtres de l'élégance moderne...

Et c'est ainsi que vous pourrez reconnaître, peut-être, au bal des facteurs ou des anciens combattants du douzième, sur le dos d'une petite danseuse, la fameuse robe de satin blanc que vous avez tant admirée sur Jeanne Helbling ou sur Marie Glory. Et l'éphémère existence des robes de conte de fées est ainsi prolongée parmi le camphre et la naphtaline, après avoir causé, non seulement de la Beauté, mais encore un peu de joie...

Suzanne Chantal.

* J'insiste sur le fait que ces ventes sont exclusivement réservées au personnel de la firme Paramount.

…s dédicacées des stars qu'il habilla.

De haut en bas :
Edwige Feuillère, Jeanne Helbing, Suzy Vernon et Chrystiane Delyne présentent des modèles d'Hubert... (Photos Paramount)

"face value" took a backseat to their suits or gowns. This was done in a rear view or a lost profile, or the face was covered at least partially by accessories, the intention being to direct attention to the clothes. Ideally, the end result was a harmonic unity in which the glamour of star and gown increased each other reciprocally.

Fit to Print

Cinema's escapist dreamworld was very effectively supported by the unimaginable wealth of magazines and other print media that, as multipliers, drew on Hollywood's endless source of complimentary visual material.[3] Film photographs relevant to fashion could be seen in both movie magazines and periodicals devoted to other topics. They were directed at "women of the world" or those who at least dreamed of becoming one. Characteristic of this are the extremely detailed descriptions often typed on the rear of press photographs. In addition to providing information about the fabrics, materials and textures, they also included extensive descriptions of the selection of colors and their highly nuanced compositions. Since the illustrations in these magazines, with the exception of the covers, were almost exclusively black and white, this information served a vital function for understanding the images.

Therefore, designs could serve as a model or inspiration for readers at a time when homemade dresses were common. As a leading cultural medium, film exercised a great deal of influence in that regard until the end of the studio system in the mid-1960s. This explains why even the sketches of Hollywood's leading costume and fashion designers were released for publication as press photographs. In order to reach their target audience, theater operators were encouraged in a leaflet – *Exhibitors Herald* – to make use of promotional material in local department stores, fashion boutiques and hairdressing salons as advertising multipliers.

An exception with regard to the color illustrations was Ektachrome. A set of large-format photographs, 8 × 10 inches, survives from the DeLuxe Color film *Désirée* (1954). The commercial intention behind this large-scale Cinemascope production was revealed by these "color slides," as the transmitted light method was expensive and normally only used for studio portraits > pp. 134–47.

> GS-90, 99, 117: THE TATTOOED LADY comes to life in the person of Gloria Swanson who wears the season's trickiest novelty -- a "tattooed" blouse -- specially created for her role in RKO Radio's new comedy, "Father Takes A Wife." Blouse is white silk jersey, the patterns done by a real tattoo artist using paint instead of a needle. Abbreviated sailor collar is white pique. Culottes are grey gabardine, cleverly cut to look like culottes in front, a skirt in back. French sailor hat is white pique crowned with a large red pompon, streamers of sailor blue grosgrain ribbon. Clip and bracelet are nautical emblems. Clogs are jersey and white pique. Amusing accessory is what Miss Swanson calls her "companion handkerchief" -- a scarf-size kerchief of fine linen, hand-hemstitched and hand-initialed -- which can be used as a scarf, to tie on a hat, bind down the hair, or just to give you something to do with your hands! Ensemble designed by Rene Hubert.

Gloria Swanson in *Father Takes a Wife* (1941), front and reverse of film still

Marilyn Monroe in *A Ticket to Tomahawk* (1950), costume test

Dorothy Gish in *Centennial Summer* (1946), costume test

Behind the Scenes

In addition to the forms of film stills described above, a certain type of photographic image was used internally and normally not intended for the public: in the field of costume design, test shots of dress rehearsals were most common. Typical examples show boards placed next to the subject on which the name of the production and scene number were chalked in. These photographs were taken either in a photography studio before shooting, in front of a neutral background or on set. They provided documentation for any reshoots and were used for future productions in a reference called the "key stills book."

While European productions commonly employed this method also, the level of regimentation and systematization was not as advanced as in Hollywood. The reasons for this were the considerably higher logistical costs and the stricter division of labor at large US studios, which produced films nonstop.[4] A series of portraits taken by the photographer Alberto Corchi of Ingrid Bergman demonstrates how this process worked. The photographs, shot in the medium format, were made into contact prints, a selection of which were then used for advertising for *Anastasia* (1956).

The Film Couturier in the Limelight

Other images for *Anastasia* have survived that can be termed photojournalism. For example, high-circulation magazines sent their own photographers to film shoots to obtain exclusive material for pre-release reporting. One such series shows Hubert in Balenciaga's studio in Paris arranging final details of a gown with the assistance of other employees from his department. Even these seemingly spontaneous photographs were posed – just as meticulously as the staging of film stills.

Classic photographic themes were somewhat more clichéd: taken in a drawing studio, tailor's workshop or costume department, they show the major film studios to be a slickly functioning "city within a city" with clear hierarchies. Hubert figured prominently in the Ektachrome photographs mentioned above also. To underscore his status as the head costume designer, he was photographed along with stars such as Jean Simmons and Merle Oberon wearing his creations. In line with his function and significance in the studio system, these photographs show him as an important figure in charge and the creative center of costume design.

Hubert worked on a total of approximately 200 productions and, after an Oscar for costume design was introduced in 1949, was nominated twice for

Anastasia (1956)

Selected advertising photograph of Ingrid Bergman, photograph by Alberto Corchi

Medium-format contact prints, photograph by Alberto Corchi

René Hubert and Ingrid Bergman during costume fittings at Atelier Balenciaga in Paris

René Hubert and seamstress at 20th Century-Fox's costume studio, 1946

his later work.[5] As a renowned film couturier he belonged to Hollywood society.[6] The active role he played in promoting himself can be seen in photographs of social events, such as those taken at the premiere of Billy Wilder's *Sunset Boulevard*, which he attended in 1950, though not as part of the production crew.

Photographs from Hubert's early years in Hollywood already reveal a great deal of self-confidence. Rather than with a needle and thread, he is portrayed with a brush and palette in reference to his training at the Académie des Beaux-Arts in Paris. In another portrait that relies wholly on his star status, his face seems disembodied in front of an indeterminate black background. Hubert looks at the camera, seemingly a transcendent thought, an idea wholly transformed into an image.

Whether with futuristic latex suits in the science fiction classic *Things to Come* (1936) or historical costumes from Napoleon's empire, fashion demonstrated its value and significance in film stills. At times it was elevated to an indispensable protagonist of and a unique selling proposition for a film production. Hubert's diverse collection of photographs provides evidence of the many ways this medium was employed in the context of a film's production. They also document the wealth of Hubert's work as a film couturier and give insight into the heyday of an industry whose primary goal was to market dreams – including those made of fabrics.

René Hubert after being contracted by Famous Players-Lasky/ Paramount, 1924, photograph by Florence Vandamm

1 See Roland Fischer-Briand, *Die Vorlust des Sehens: Betrachtungen zur Filmauswertungsfotografie aus der Fotosammlung des Österreichischen Filmmuseums. Entwicklung – Typologie – Verwendung*, master's thesis, Donau Universität Krems, 2006.
2 Joel W. Finler, *Hollywood Movie Stills: The Golden Age*, London, 1995, p. 43.
3 Guy Hennebelle listed 500 twentieth century movie magazines published beginning in the 1920s, primarily in the West and some of them with enormous circulations. See *Les revues du cinéma dans le monde*, ed. Guy Hennebelle, *CinémAction*, no. 69, 1993.
4 Jan-Christopher Horak, *Dream Merchants: Making and Selling Hollywood's Golden Age*, Rochester, NY, 1989, pp. 14ff.
5 *Désirée*, directed by Henry Coster, USA, 1954; *The Visit*, directed by Bernhard Wicki, USA/FR/DE/IT, 1965.
6 His homosexuality was studiously ignored, another indication of his social standing in the film industry. See William J. Mann, *Behind the Screen: How Gays and Lesbians Shaped Hollywood, 1910–1969*, New York, 2001, p. 42.

Gloria Swanson, René Hubert, Swanson's daughter Michelle Farmer and Robert Wagner at the premiere of *Sunset Boulevard* (1950) in New York

Merle Oberon and René Hubert at costume fittings for *Désirée* (1954)

Portrait of René Hubert, 1930s

Costumes in Ektachrome

***Désirée* (1954, directed by Henry Koster), Oscar nomination for Best Costume Design in a color film**
pp. 134–147: Approximately half of Jean Simmons' costumes and screen tests in order of appearance in film

“It is odd to have to record that the outstanding star of [the] show […] should be a certain René Hubert, whose name appeared in the programme after those of all the lesser performers. But it is a fact that Hubert’s decor and costumes, particularly costumes, were the prettiest and the wittiest things, in the whole show.”

The News Chronicle, 1938

René Hubert and the Stage

Angelo Luerti

René Hubert was one of the most talented and versatile costume designers from the 1920s to the 1960s. He contributed to nearly fifty shows, including those by George Black, Erik Charell, Duke Ellington, Leslie Henson, Edwin Lester, Eric Maschwitz and Ralph Reader, in addition to providing his artistic contributions to dozens of films. With his vivid imagination, the unusual flair for color and glamorous effects, he has led many shows to become legendary and synonymous with extravagance.

Hubert made his debut in Paris by designing, with Umberto Brunelleschi and Couderc, a few costumes for the revue *De Toutes les Couleurs* (January 1922) at the Ba-ta-Clan, directed by Bénédicte Rasimi. The sumptuousness of the costumes she supplied earned the Ba-ta-Clan, the prestigious title of "Temple des merveilles." Rasimi possessed an extraordinary eye. Queen of good taste and elegance, her perfection in the art of costume was rarely equaled.[1] It was Rasimi who promoted his debut on the recommendation of her son, a longtime friend of Hubert, after having been favorably impressed by his sensitivity for colors and shapes and his talent for glamorous effects.

In this revue Rasimi herself, after the curtain rose, entered the scene in a chariot pulled by twenty graceful girls in skirts with cubist motifs. "The blues, purples and reds of the skirts, the fiery color of the bustiers and the white collars brought enthusiastic comments from the public for the apparently contrasting combinations but done in a way to attain effects both refined and highly suggestive"[2] – skills that Hubert learned very well and made his own throughout his long career.

Freelancing across the Atlantic

Before getting his first credit as a costume designer, Hubert had tried his luck in 1920 in New York, where his sketches were greatly appreciated by Lee Shubert, a Broadway entrepreneur and head of the largest

Design for *An Alle*, Grosses Schauspielhaus, Berlin (1925), program

Design for *L'Auberge du Cheval Blanc*, Théâtre Mogador, Paris (1932)

US theater empire in the twentieth century > p. 161. He charged Hubert with doing some costuming and scenery for the shows *Kissing Time* (Lyric Theatre, October 1920), *June Love* (Knickerbocker Theatre, April 1921) and *Princess Virtue* (Central Theatre, May 1921). Back in Paris, Hubert designed for *Ziegfeld Follies of 1922* (Shubert's New Amsterdam Theatre, June 1922). On the other side of the Atlantic Ocean, Hubert also freelanced for Bénédicte Rasimi's atelier in Paris. On her request he designed costumes for several theaters at least until 1925, including four shows dated 1921 for the *Théâtre de La Chauve-Souris* > pp. 164–65. In all these cases, however, his contributions were uncredited.

Having returned once again from New York, where he had been hired as historical consultant for the film *Monsieur Beaucaire* (1924), he found only a few job opportunities in Paris, including designing the costumes for one scene out of forty-five ("Connais-tu le pays?") for *Vive la Femme!* (Palace, October 1924) with Maurice Chevalier. The following year he designed, with José de Zamora, Jean Aumond and Madeleine Vilpelle, just a few sumptuous costumes for *La revue très excitante* and *Archi nue* (Concert Mayol, January 1925), starring the famous diseuse Dora Stroeva.

In Berlin he found another small but interesting opportunity, designing for the revue *An Alle* (Grosses Schauspielhaus, October 1924). The aim of its producer, Erik Charell, was to present enchanting dancing girls with divine legs to show that revues made in Berlin could be "as contemporary as the jazz band that turns the Siegmund-yodeling and Siegfried-screeching to laughter."[3] The cast included the famous Tiller Girls, a group from London much loved by Hitler for its synchronism. Costume and set design were by Ernst Stern, except for three out of twenty scenes by Hubert: "Orangenernte in Californien" (Orange Harvest in California), "Unter dem Florentinerhut" (Under the Florentine Hat) and "Das goldene Lied – Ein Hymnus auf das Gold und die Liebe" (The Golden Song: a Hymn to Gold and Love).[4]

Hubert was now twenty-nine years old – an age at which his contemporaries had long since reached the peak of their careers, whereas he could boast only a few marginal acknowledgments. The difficulty of finding work in a market dominated by the best European designers such as Georges Barbier, Umberto Brunelleschi, Ladislaus Czettel, Charles Gesmar, Dolly Tree and José de Zamora, to name a few,[5] induced him to work as a fashion stylist for Jean Patou and other tailors of Rue de la Paix. Moreover, the exponential growth of cinemas caused a music hall crisis by reducing audience numbers. In the darkest moment of his career, he seized an opportunity that radically changed his life: the meeting with Gloria Swanson, one of the most famous actresses of the silent movies, in fall 1924, while she was in Paris to prepare for the film *Madame Sans-Gêne*.[6]

From then on, Hubert would design mainly for films while always keeping contact with the stages in the cities where he stayed. The dazzling costumes for *The Love Song* (Century Theatre, New York, January 1925), a gorgeous Jacques Offenbach operetta with a cast of over 250, were by "Hubert of Paris." The play was a tremendous success: "No more splendid a welcome to any stage performance could be imagined than that which was accorded to *The Love Song* on the opening last night."[7] In early 1928 Hubert returned to Europe to work for the producer Erich Pommer at Universum Film (Ufa) in Berlin. The new show by Erik Charell at the Grosses Schauspielhaus, *Im weissen Rössl* (November 1930), was again designed by Ernst Stern. Hubert contributed only "modern clothing" for one of the sixteen scenes[8] >pp. 170–71. The show was banned in National Socialist Germany due to its Jewish coauthors.

Working for the film director René Clair in Paris, Hubert designed one out of sixty scenes ("La Mode Féminine") for *Nuit de Folies* (Folies Bergère, February 1932) and the "Costumes bleus du ballet" for *L'Auberge du Cheval Blanc* (Mogador, October 1932), which staged 881 times. While in Paris he also designed for the London musical comedy *Here's How!* (The Saville Theatre, February 1934), starring George Robey, one of the greatest music hall performers, and the French-born film star Lili Damita. The tasteful costumes by Hubert were "as little as possible" since the action took place in a nudist camp.

Stage Hits in London

Having lost his Hollywood contract with Fox Film, after its merger with Twentieth Century Pictures to become 20th Century-Fox in early 1935, Hubert was called to London by Alexander Korda, a British film producer.[9] Thanks to the fame acquired in the field of cinema, his upcoming arrival in London immediately aroused great deal of interest among theatrical producers who did not take long to offer him to design for entire plays. It was the beginning for Hubert of a period of intense work for both the cinema and a lengthy list of stage hits.

Madge Elliott and Edna Best in *Cinderella*, London Coliseum, London (1936)

Binnie Hale says goodbye to St. Agatha's School, *Rise and Shine*, Theatre Royal, Drury Lane, London (1936), photograph by Stage Photos Ltd.

He started with *Cinderella* at the London Coliseum (December 1936), one of the most popular stories performed in English-speaking countries, especially during the year-end season. The 900 designs necessary to produce the 3,000 costumes of the pantomime took three months' work and were done in spring 1935, eighteen months before the opening: "It is the most artistically dressed and staged pantomime I have seen during a long experience. The costumes of René Hubert are really beautiful...."[10] "Everything is in excellent artistic taste, from the beautiful scenic and costume effects designed by Alick Johnstone and René Hubert respectively, to the picturesque and romantic dances."[11]

He went on with musical comedies at Drury Lane. This theater was known for its lavish productions by the same Ralph Reader responsible for *Cinderella*, with large casts and extravagant set pieces living up to its reputation as a place of spectacular technical wizardry, such as a helicopter taking off from the stage of *Rise and Shine,* an earthquake in *Careless Rapture* and a train crash in *Crest of a Wave.*

The musical comedy *Rise and Shine* (May 1936) starred Binnie Hale, one of the most successful musical theater stars in London. Ten days before the opening, as was its tradition, Drury Lane heralded its return with a gigantic dress parade of the costumes for this show: "There were 300 mannequins over 1,000 costumes, and the show lasted 12 hours.... The dresses are a combination of Hungarian, Austrian and Hollywood. The remarkable thing is that Hubert has made no two costumes alike. This is the first musical show in which every member of the chorus is dressed differently in every scene. For the scene of the Garden Party, Hubert bought 18,000 yards of organdie. For the cape in a palace scene, he had to obtain 1,500 yards of white satin.... The girls' dresses are full of brilliant and amusing ideas.... There are smart little divided skirts, sleeves starched at the top to give the wide shoulder...."[12] "Girls were wearing trousered skirts in every color. Some had trousers with blue sashes; others had horizon blue and white trousers and jaunty little hats to match.... The boys were dreams in gray toppers, gray morning suits and white gloves.... Big velvet hats like cartwheels and velvet ribbons which tie under the chin were other new fashions designed to captivate women."[13] The spectacular musical comedy had a notable triumph thanks in part to the big crowds, the chorus effects, the ballets and the dance ensembles.

The following play at Drury Lane was the first of two musical extravaganzas by the very popular composer and actor Ivor Novello: *Careless Rapture*

Ivor Novello, Dorothy Dickson and ensemble in *Careless Rapture*, Theatre Royal, Drury Lane, London (1936)

(September 1936), also starring Dorothy Dickson. The musical was not only a superb spectacle, it possessed every ingredient to delight a lover of musical entertainment: a melodious score, two elaborate ballets and lovely costumes by Hubert, "one of the most widely experienced and interesting personalities of his profession"[14] > pp. 176–77. *Crest of the Wave* (September 1937), the second Novello musical, was seen by nearly half a million people in a seven-month run.

Over the same months Hubert designed for three shows at the Gaiety Theatre produced by the comedian Leslie Henson and his business partner, the writer Firth Shephard. *Swing Along* (September 1936) starred Henson, famous for his bulging eyes, malleable face and raspy voice; Louise Browne, a dancer and musical comedy star; Fred Emney, a character actor and comedian; and Richard Hearne, a comic actor. They all became part of a regular company. "René Hubert costumes rank among the daintiest seen at the Gaiety in recent years."[15] The excellent all-around entertainment that combined music, dancing and humor was followed by *Going Greek* (September 1937), a musical comedy cast with the entire Gaiety Theatre team. "The costumes and the sets by René Hubert are less garish than in most musical comedies and therefore more kind to the eye."[16] The third show by Henson was *Running Riot* (August 1938) with the same cast of *Going Greek*. "I liked very much indeed the colourful costumes with which René Hubert decorated all the members of the cast and enhanced the beauty of a chorus which needed little enhancing."[17]

During the same period Eric Maschwitz, a successful English entertainer and writer, commissioned designs for three musical comedies, beginning with *Balalaika* (The Adelphi Theatre, December 1936). "This production is one of the most beautiful, spectacular shows I have seen for many years.... Truly lovely are the gorgeous costumes by René Hubert, and the setting by Leon Davey are a fitting background."[18] Then it was the turn of *Paprika* (His Majesty's Theatre, September 1938). Hubert's costumes won general admiration: "Programme notes inform us how much care has been taken to make the costumes as authentic as possible. René Hubert [...] tells us that he has tried in the cafe clothes and ball dresses of act two to conjure up the worldly Budapest of 1887 in an age of unruffled happiness and prosperity."[19]

Leslie Henson, Louise Browne and ensemble in *Swing Along*, Gaiety Theatre, London (1936)

Darling You (Streatham Hill Theatre, March 1937), a spectacular musical comedy by Prince Littler, starred Britain's famous comedian Leslie Fuller, known as "the rubber-faced comedian." "The dresses are picturesque and blend effectively by René Hubert."[20] "The appeal of this kind of entertainment, is to the eye and ear.... The eye was charmed by a dazzling display of colour [...] the dresses of the play's innumerable dancers designed with an artist's eye...."[21]

Hubert also designed for *New Faces* (Metropolitan, June 1937) by Janice Hart and Frank O'Brian. Together with John Lawrence they formed a trio responsible for a great amount of laughter. "Its spectacular scenes are far more originally and attractively staged than is usually the case; indeed, one doubts whether any revue that has visited Walthamstow has had such colourful settings to show. The spectacular portions of the revue are well represented by 'The Ballet of Flags,' 'Ladies in Lace' and 'The Circus,' all of which are delightful to the eye.... The Casino girls, who make several appearances in a variety of costumes, help greatly."[22] Later came *Floodlight* (Saville Theatre, June 1937), whose "best of the scenes [...] is called 'Prelude to Battle,' a stage spectacle in brilliant costumes and uniforms of the Duchess of Richmond's Waterloo ball at Brussels in 1815."[23] "A feature of the revue is the exquisite decor by René Hubert who is also responsible for the colourful and lovely dresses."[24]

George Black, the impresario initiator of the Crazy Gang revues, produced *London Rhapsody* (The London Palladium, September 1937), one of his largest variety shows. It starred the Crazy Gang, a team of six British entertainers who achieved considerable domestic popularity. It is a lively affair in many gorgeous scenes labeled after various phases of London life past and present. But the entertainment could not easily be anything less than breezy and high spirited with the Crazy Gang, the life and breath of the show. The revue was considered to be one of the most spectacular shows ever produced at the Palladium, a mixture of color and spectacle, ingenious tricks of staging and straight variety acts. The costumes for the six visually richest scenes were created by Michel Gyarmathy and Lucien Bertaux, Ladislaus Czettel, Estelle Revolg, Alec Shanks, Ernst Stern and René Hubert, whose contribution was for "A Mayfair Salon," a scene with Harry Dennis' Dancing Dudes' waltz "Along the River with You." It ran for more than 500 performances. A contemporary critic noted, "Whereas Ivor Novello has put Drury Lane back on the map by altering the standard of production

London Rhapsody, The London Palladium (1937)

there to a point far removed from the theatre's traditions, George Black has achieved the same results at the Palladium by a different process."[25]

The following year brought *Pelissier's Follies of 1938* (Saville Theatre, May 1938), a lively revue with costumes by Hubert "in a style that pays full homage to the West End."[26] Two musical comedies followed at the Prince's Theatre, starting with Douglas Furber's *Wild Oats* (April 1938). "It is odd to have to record that the outstanding star of a show whose cast included Sydney Howard, Vera Pearce and Arthur Riscoe should be a certain René Hubert, whose name appeared in the programme after those of all the lesser performers. But it is a fact that Hubert's decor and costumes, particularly costumes, were the prettiest and the wittiest things, in the whole show."[27] "The exquisite beauty of the dresses and decor by René Hubert. Not for a long time has the West End stage seen anything so lovely as these pastels run riot."[28] *Sitting Pretty* (August 1939) starred Sydney Howard, who had proved so popular in *Wild Oats*. Set and costumes were by Leon Davey and Hubert, who "have collaborated on dressing a number of sumptuous musicals of recent years, and their names are a guarantee that *Sitting Pretty* will at least delight the eye."[29] The revue was interrupted after fifteen performances due to the outbreak of the war.

Los Angeles near Hollywood

In those busy days Hubert also spent time in his native Switzerland, designing fashion for the National Exhibition held in Zurich in 1939. The fashion shows *Der verlorene Faden* (May), *Alles neu* (July) and *Eve* (September) were presented as cabaret programs and earned him notoriety nationwide.[30] Unable to return to London because of the war, on November 14 he embarked in Genoa for the United States on a steamship flying the Italian flag, a choice dictated by the fact that Italy was still neutral in the conflict. Back in Los Angeles, Hubert started freelance designing for Hollywood films.

He was hired for the "highly intellectual [...] but entertaining"[31] expensive production *Jump for Joy* (Mayan Theatre, July 1941), an "all-Negro" sophisticated musical starring Duke Ellington and his orchestra with the beauteous and vivacious Dorothy Dandridge. Contrary to other all African American revues of the time, it was very outspoken on racial matters > pp. 174–75. It was a proud, satirical revue that blasted racial stereotypes, perhaps too far ahead of its time. The production team received protestations and death threats. Right before the finale, the Sharp Easter scene opened with the whole cast promenading in pastel (expressionistic) costumes designed by Hubert. "The girls were absolutely stunning. At the end of the parade came the tailors dressed in gold and purple [...] leading Potts [...] in the loudest, most outrageous checkered suit ever constructed.... The house fell down."[32] The show lasted for only 101 performances. Duke Ellington described it later in his life as "the first 'social significance' show.... It never made it to Broadway, but it made it to history."[33] It was unable to move on from Los Angeles because of the United States' involvement in World War II.

In November 1942 Hubert landed at 20th Century-Fox, where he stayed until the end of the decade. While in Los Angeles he designed the costumes for three operettas at the local Civic Light Opera by impresario Edwin Lester, who worked in collaboration with the San Francisco Civic Light Opera to begin with *Rosalinda* (San Francisco, April 1947), adapted from the Max Reinhardt–Erich Korngold version of Johann Strauss' operetta classic *Die Fledermaus*. "Rosalinda has been decked out like a frosted cake as a show of spectacular beauty. And the ladies of the ensemble, gowned in yards and yards of satin and tulle, look like spun sugar candy."[34] *The Three Musketeers* (Los Angeles, June 1947), with glittering costumes by Walter J. Israel (men) and Hubert (women), and *Naughty Marietta* (Los Angeles, May 1948), starring Susanna Foster (Marietta), who "wears Hubert's clothes in a very captivating way,"[35] followed. First performed in 1910, it had endured in popularity over the decades, becoming a staple of musical theater companies across the globe.

Back in Switzerland

Feeling uneasy over the continuing attacks on homosexuals (like him) during the McCarthy era, Hubert left Los Angeles around 1950 and settled in St. Gallen, only returning to the United States from time to time for selected projects. In this late phase of his career he mainly designed for contemporary interpretations of classic plays from previous centuries. On the occasion of its 150th jubilee the Stadttheater St. Gallen staged Wolfgang Amadeus Mozart's *Così fan tutte* (November 1955). Supported by an exceptionally high budget, including for the costumes, Hubert made extensive use of the textiles sponsored by the internationally renowned local companies Stoffel and Forster Willi, for which he had been working as a textile designer.[36] Toward the end of the decade the Schweizerische Verkehrszentrale

Wolfgang Amadeus Mozart's opera *Così fan tutte*, Stadttheater St. Gallen (1955), fabrics from textile companies Forster Willi & Co. and Stoffel & Cie

Geschwister Schmid (Trio Shmeed) in *Swiss Echoes*, Radio City Music Hall, New York (1959)

promoted a show with the Geschwister Schmid – well known in the United States as Trio Shmeed – at Radio City Music Hall in New York: *Swiss Echoes* (April 1959) was presented four times a day for four weeks and seen by over six hundred thousand Americans.

Residing in Zurich from 1960 on, Hubert designed for *The Merry Widow*, an operetta by Franz Lehár, in a new gay, young, fresh and bright version at the Los Angeles Civic Light Opera, again produced by Edwin Lester (April 1961): "Costumes drew audible comments of awe from the audience.... Patrice Munsel (as the Merry Widow) in a gown that would make a queen envious...."[37] Three years later he designed the same operetta at Lincoln Center (August 1964), again with Munsel in the title role, as a last New York production: "The costuming by René Hubert utilized the traditional huge plumed hats and hour-glass gowns, designing them in rich colours and materials. The can-can dancers in the scene of Maxim's were cute puff-balls of brightly hued skirts and black lace stockings."[38]

The commissions for Hubert's final stage designs came from Herbert Graf, a former longtime producer at New York's Metropolitan Opera. Having settled in Switzerland, Graf initially worked at the Stadttheater Zürich and subsequently at the Grand Théâtre de Genève. Hubert designed costumes for Johann Strauss' *Die Fledermaus* (Stadttheater, December 1961),[39] followed by Giuseppe Verdi's *La Traviata* (Grand Théâtre, September 1963) and, at the age of seventy, *La Chauve-Souris* (Grand Théâtre, December 1965), again based on the operetta by Strauss. "When the corps de ballet, under the orders of Serge Golovine, in classic white and black outfits, launched with all its stars into the twists and turns of the famous waltz *Le beau Danube bleu*, it was delirium!"[40] With its restaging in May 1970, René Hubert's long and very intense career finally ended – a career that flourished on many stages throughout Europe and the United States.

Recovering the individual theatrical productions Hubert has put his stamp on has not been easy. Even less so would it be to speak of his artistic contributions, given the lack of their visual recordings. For this reason we have considered it appropriate to leave this task to those critics who have had the privilege of viewing these shows.

1 Angelo Luerti, *Non solo Erté = Not only Erté: Costume Design for the Paris Music Hall 1918-1940*, Vicenza, 2006.
2 Luerti, *Erté*.
3 Alfred Flechtheim, "Vom Ballett zur Revue," *Der Querschnitt* (1924).
4 The revue was also staged at the Ronacher Theater in Vienna, March 1925.
5 Luerti, *Erté*.
6 See the contribution by Elisabeth Bronfen in this book.
7 *The Brooklyn Daily Eagle*, January 14, 1925.
8 The program does not mention on which scene he collaborated. The revue was also staged at the Schauspielhaus in Vienna, September 1931.
9 See the contribution by Amy Sargeant in this book.
10 *Aberdeen Press*, December 26, 1936.
11 *The Stage*, December 31, 1936.
12 *The News Chronicle*, April 28, 1936.
13 *Daily Herald*, April 28, 1936.
14 *The Era*, May 12, 1938.
15 *The Stage*, September 10, 1936.
16 *Western Morning News*, September 20, 1937.
17 *The News Chronicle*, September 1, 1938.
18 *The Daily Independent*, December 24, 1936.
19 *The Stage*, September 22, 1938. It ran for only eleven performances and was then performed as *Magyar Melody* at His Majesty's Theatre, January 1939.
20 *The Stage*, November 19, 1936.
21 *The Scotsman*, January 26, 1937.
22 *The Stage*, September 30, 1937.
23 *The Stage*, July 1, 1937.
24 *The Rebus*, November 5, 1937.
25 J. J. Kennedy, *The Man Who Wrote the Teddy Bears' Picnic*, AuthorHouse, 2011.
26 *The Bystander*, May 18, 1938.
27 *The News Chronicle* (London), April 14, 1938.
28 *Reynolds's Newspaper*, April 17, 1938.
29 *The News Chronicle* (London), July 28, 1939.
30 See the contribution by Katharina Tietze in this book.
31 Edward Kennedy "Duke" Ellington, *Duke Ellington: Music Is My Mistress*, Garden City, 1973, p. 176.
32 John Franceschina, *Duke Ellington's Music for the Theatre*, Jefferson, 2001 (2017), p. 207. Scenery and lighting were also by Hubert. Potts Jackson was a member of the cast.
33 David Johnson, *Jump for Joy: Duke Ellington's Celebratory Musical*, 2008, https://indianapublicmedia.org/nightlights/jump-for-joy-duke-ellingtons-celebratory-musical.php.
34 *Hollywood Citizen*, May 20, 1947.
35 *The News Chronicle*, June 1, 1948.
36 See the contribution by Katharina Tietze in this book.
37 *Pasadena Independent*, April 19, 1961.
38 *The Stage*, September 17, 1964.
39 Also staged at the Teatro dell'Opera di Roma as *Il Pipistrello*, January 1962.
40 *Le Nouvelliste*, December 29, 1965.

Johann Strauss' *Die Fledermaus*, Stadttheater Zürich (1961), ensemble scene and design

New York – Paris – Berlin – London – Los Angeles

Unknown stage, presumably New York
p. 161: design for unknown play, 1920

Unknown music hall, presumably Paris
pp. 162/163: designs for unknown play, 1921

***Théâtre de la Chauve-Souris,* Théâtre Femina, Paris (Nikita Balieff)**
pp. 164/165: designs for unknown play, 1921

Jewel ballet in unknown play, costumed by Berlin company Hugo Baruch & Cie
p. 166: design for "Emerald," 1922
p. 167: design for "Ruby," 1922

Flag ballet in unknown play, presumably costumed by Berlin company Hugo Baruch & Cie
p. 168: design for "The Flags," 1922
p. 169: design for "The Bells," 1922

***Im weissen Rössl*, Grosses Schauspielhaus, Berlin (1930, Erik Charell)**
pp. 170/171: designs

Unknown play, presumably London or Paris
p. 172: design for "Chinese Girl No. 6," n.d.
p. 173: design for "Chinese Girl No. 11," n.d.

***Jump for Joy,* Mayan Theatre, Los Angeles (1941, Duke Ellington)**
p. 174: Duke Ellington and band, program cover
p. 175: ensemble and designs, program, double pages

***Careless Rapture,* Theatre Royal, Drury Lane, London (1936, Leontine Sagan, Ralph Reader)**
pp. 176/177: Dorothy Dickson and ensemble

32
Mis Dial
41 E 30
Phone
Madison Square
8185 -
René 1920.

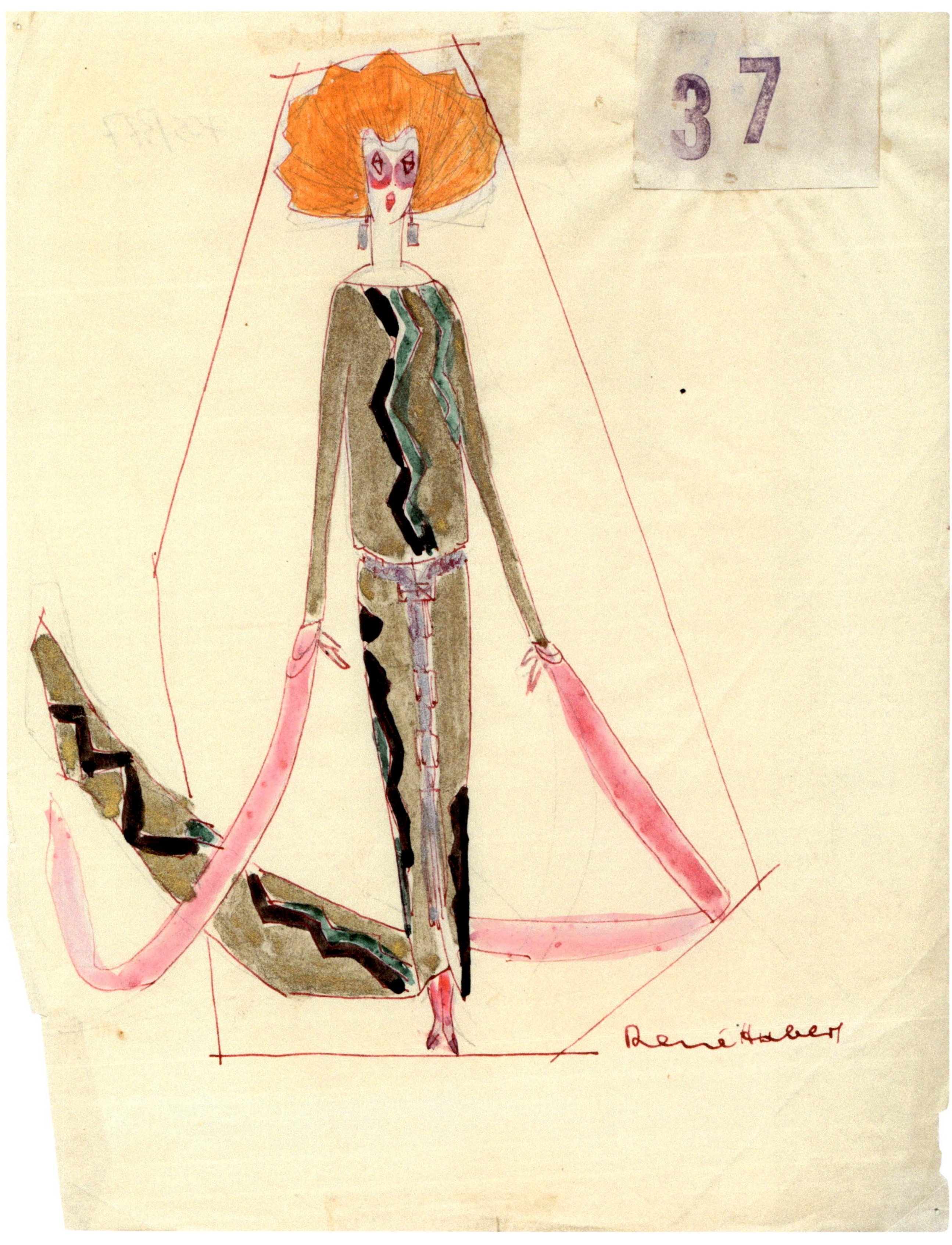
37
René Hubert

37
les monokles
René Hubert
1921

René
Hubert

1921

29274.
Edelstein-Ballet
Smaragd
Hugo Baruch & Cie
Berlin

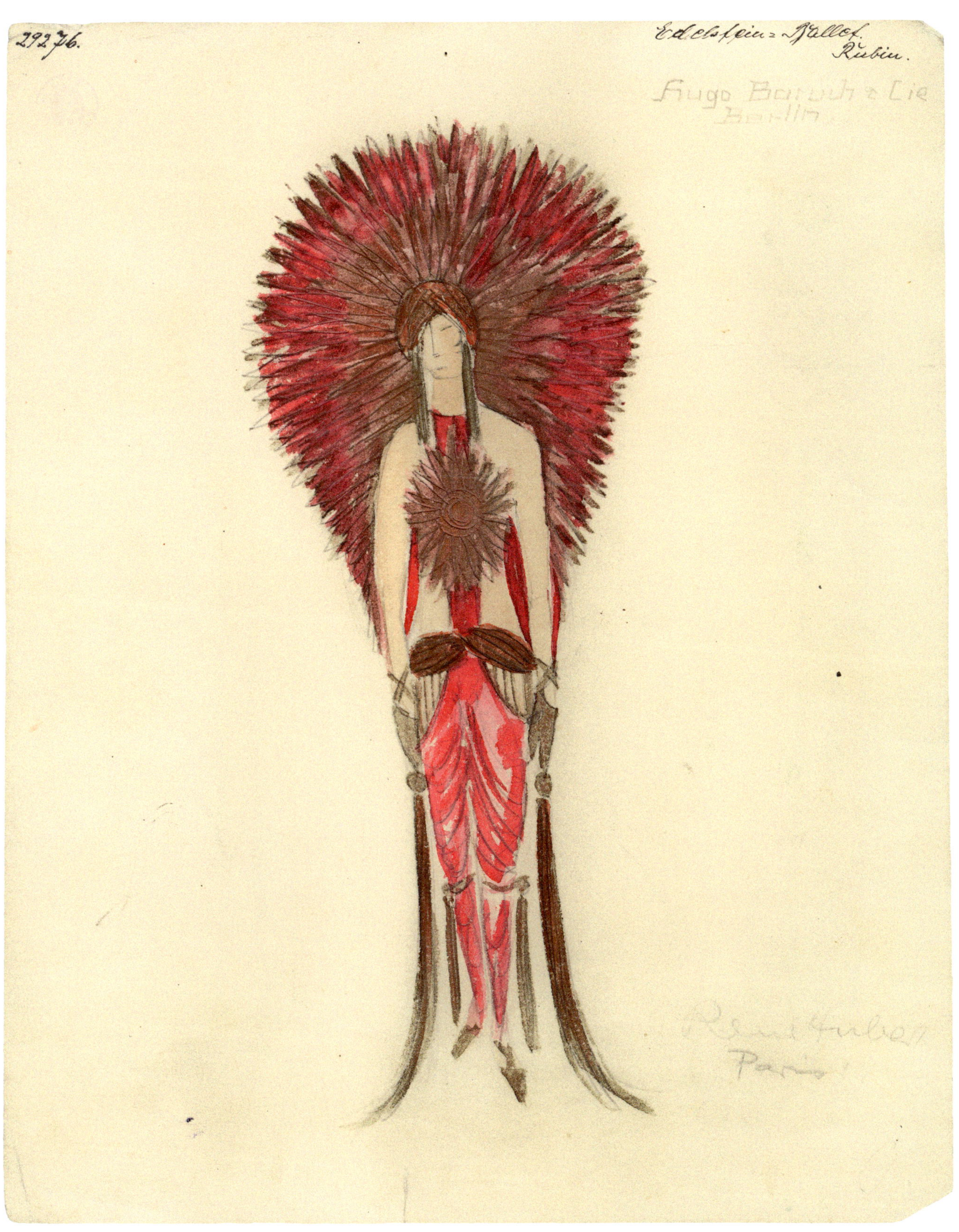
29276.
Edelstein=Ballet.
Rubin.
Hugo Baruch & Cie
Berlin

36353.
7
Die Flaggen
lose einzelne Flaggen wild fliegend
René Hubert
1922

36358.
Die Glocken.
René Hubert
1932

light
and slit
open
skirt

JUMP for JOY

FOR

Costumes by Rene Hubert

"It's better to have one or two dresses that harmonize with the hat, shoes and handbag than a full closet with none of the little things that make a modern woman and demonstrate good grooming and care."

René Hubert, 1927

"Our Famous Countryman": René Hubert and Fashion

Katharina Tietze

Film and Fashion

In the 1930s film and fashion were closely intertwined. Film costumes started fashion trends, and large numbers of copies were sold.[1] Hollywood's film industry produced stars who were in the limelight and required an appropriate personal wardrobe. René Hubert played an important role in this system: he designed costumes and fashion for major stars, creating glamour both on screen and off. He had a fine sense of sensational, elegant appearances; was a good and fast draftsman; had a charming personality; was formidable at networking; and was also extremely productive.

Hubert designed both film costumes and dresses for Gloria Swanson for many years. There was an anecdote involving Marlene Dietrich he often recounted: in 1937 he brought some hats to London for her when returning from Paris. When he unpacked them, she claimed that she was not able to try them on immediately, then disappeared into an adjoining room and returned topless. She tried on one after another, saying, "You know, this is the only way I can see how they look with a plunging neckline."[2] In a charming letter addressed to "dear René," she wrote, "I would like terribly much to have a few dresses made. It would be sweet of you to come up with a cocktail dress with a jacket in a spare hour."[3] Several sketches that have survived were then sent to Dietrich with swatches for her private wardrobe. For the two evening gowns he skillfully played with classic forms for the jacket and daring necklines.

For films produced in London or Paris, Hubert often had costumes made at prestigious fashion boutiques. Costumes worn by Ingrid Bergman in *Anastasia* (1956), for example, were tailored by Balenciaga. Hubert met the renowned fashion designer at Zurich's Kronenhalle restaurant – run by silk dealer Gustav Zumsteg's mother – and was given permission to use his studio.[4] The costumes for *The Visit*

Design for Marlene Dietrich's personal wardrobe, n.d.

(1964), made at Rome's Studio Cinecittà and starring Bergman, were tailored at Nina Ricci in Paris. The fashion photographer Fortunato Scrimali shot portraits of the star in her film wardrobe for the Italian magazine *Epoca* >pp. 198–205.[5] Differentiating between a film costume and fashion is difficult when presented in this way. The actor, although forty-eight years old at the time, was as attractive as a model and mastered the appropriate poses. Still, this involved two different things: in the adaptation of Dürrenmatt's *The Visit* the protagonist showed off her wealth when returning to the village of her birth. This is about a character and the importance of her clothing.

The close link between film and fashion was also recognized in Switzerland, and quarterly special issues of the periodical *Schweizer Film Zeitung,* titled *Film-Mode,* began appearing in 1941. In the first Hubert was described as "Hollywood's fashion king";[6] he was in a sense its inspiration and appeared again and again. In 1947 he commented on "fashion in Hollywood," repeatedly pointing out the accentuation of the waist and the figure in general. Furthermore, he claimed that "Even historical costumes must be adapted more or less to modern tastes. [...] But that they still breathe the atmosphere of their time and are right for the film's style, the role's character and the actor's personality, you see, that is the special task of the costume designer."[7]

Not only is this true for historical films, but it also clearly shows the differences between a film costume and a privately owned dress. When Hubert worked for Les Studios Paramount in Joinville, near Paris, the French film magazine *Pour Vous* wrote the following in 1932: "René Hubert and everyone who has dealt with the problem of putting fashion on the screen believe that a model designed for the studio and adapted perfectly to the requirements of cinema cannot be worn in the city, just as the most charming dress normally does not bring anything to the screen."[8] One of the most well-known fashion designers of all time, Coco Chanel, made a disappointing attempt as a costume designer for Gloria Swanson in the Hollywood production *Tonight or Never* (1931). After that Swanson had Hubert satisfy her needs again.

Marlene Dietrich in *Shanghai Express* (1932), autographed photograph dedicated to René Hubert

The National Exhibition

The fact that Hubert, after working in Paris, Berlin, London, New York and Hollywood, made contacts in his home country resulted primarily from one event: the 1939 Swiss National Exhibition in Zurich. In his memoirs he claimed that it took some time before he understood what a certain Herr Schuppisser of Zurich wanted from him on the telephone.[9] The idea of a fashion theater in a space the architect Karl Egender designed for this purpose was, in fact, unique. A group of Swiss fashion and textile manufacturers, encouraged by boutique owner Edgar Grieder, put on three shows. Models were trained and important figures in Switzerland's entertainment industry were hired. And then they thought of two famous countrymen who were abroad, Robert Piguet and, most importantly, Hubert.

An article about him that appeared in the daily newspaper *Neue Zürcher Zeitung* in 1937 probably played a role in this. It ended with the words "It might be possible to once again convince this internationally successful artist to participate in a production or at least an exhibition in his home country."[10] An opportunity presented itself, the 1939 National Exhibition, and so some first-class participants were included in the realization of an original idea.

At the first meeting Hubert criticized the existing ideas as being too firmly based in folklore; personally, he had "extremely modern costumes with sex appeal" in mind.[11] After his suggestions were accepted, he designed dresses for the short scenes, which were dedicated to such companies as Bally, Grieder and Stoffel. The costumes were then produced by Gaby Jouval; the partner of her Zurich haute couture salon was Wilhelm Schuppisser, mentioned above. In his autobiography Hubert describes this euphorically as the "most wonderful experience of my life."[12]

This successful collaboration led to a number of interesting commissions. First, Hubert was hired for the Swiss Pavilion at the 1940 World's Fair in New York. Dresses that he designed were displayed there on mechanical mannequins, an invention that had been created for the fashion pavilion at the 1939 National Exhibition.

He worked for the shoe company Bally repeatedly as a consultant, for example developing the idea of a portico as a background for the presentation of footwear at Mustermesse Basel, a trade fair where Swiss companies displayed their products. In 1948 he prepared Studio Treize, an exclusive salon near Zurich's Bahnhofstrasse where Bally presented new shoe styles and models.[13] This clearly shows that Hubert was both regarded as a designer of dresses and was also in demand as a glamour expert. Even the setup of his space for fittings in Hollywood was carefully planned: "I tried to create in it a Parisian atmosphere with of course a great deal of Hollywood

Show *Der verlorene Faden*, fashion theater, Swiss National Exhibition, 1939, Zurich, *Zürcher Illustrierte*, cover, photograph by © Gotthard Schuh/Fotostiftung Schweiz

Studio Treize shoe shop for Bally company, Zurich, 1948

Shows in fashion theater, Swiss National Exhibition, 1939, Zurich

Top: "Heel in the Snow," organdy fabric by Heberlein & Co., shoes by Bally

Bottom: clothing for the modern woman

show. The room – quite big – was all in gray: Light gray walls – deeper gray carpet – gray duvet sofa in over dimensional Louis XV style that came out of a set of a former décor with a few bergières and chairs to match. And of course, all in mirrors and some other great three-panel mirrors for the fitting. Some lovely flower arrangement by the studio gardener gave the whole room certain elegance."[14]

Designs for the Textile Industry

Hubert began drawing fashion at an early stage in his career. The Berlin magazine *Styl: Blätter für Mode und die angenehmen Dinge des Lebens* published his sketch of a dress by the local boutique Hammer. This is possibly how he met the journalist Elsa Herzog; he illustrated her article about Paris fashion in the periodical *Sport im Bild* that same year.

Beginning in 1950, when he moved back to Switzerland permanently, Hubert designed fabrics and occasionally dresses for Stoffel & Co.[15] The company, based in St. Gallen, specialized in cotton fabrics and had approximately one thousand employees in 1960.[16] This contact also came about due to his involvement in the 1939 National Exhibition. "Our famous countryman" also sketched dresses, inspired by the fabrics he had designed, for the magazine *Film-Mode* mentioned above[17] > pp. 192–197. This contribution showed the close connection between fabrics and dresses, and also provided evidence of what a talented draftsman Hubert was. It was no coincidence that he devoted himself to textile design in Switzerland: the country had an international reputation in this field, while Paris was still regarded as the most important location for fashion design.

In 1954 a "Letter from Los Angeles" appeared in the periodical *Schweizer Textilien*. It contained a report on the US fashion designer Pat Premo and her latest summer dresses using Swiss fabrics: "Her most important foreign supplier is Stoffel & Cie, whose famed creator, René Hubert, collaborates closely with Miss Premo. The freedom granted Hubert benefits the US company; many of the unique ideas he permits himself to explore are the kind of things that Miss Premo loves the most."[18]

Hubert decorated a special event in 1955: a fashion show was held in St. Gallen at its equestrian sports event, and he contributed a number of models. Shown are elegant dresses with narrow waistlines and flowing skirts as well as tight-fitting costumes in the style of the New Look. Photographs from

Illustration for Berlin fashion boutique Hammer, 1922

Fabric designed by René Hubert for St. Gallen textile company Stoffel & Cie, dress made by California fashion designer Pat Premo, 1954

René Hubert with model wearing a dress for Stoffel & Cie, fashion show at St. Gallen's equestrian sports event, 1955

Hubert's estate, with "Stoffel & Cie Photo Album" stamped on the back and dated 1955, show similar models > pp. 189-91. That same year an advertisement announced a fashion show "of models with Stoffel fabrics, created by René Hubert, Hollywood" at Jelmoli department store.[19] For the same business he designed raincoats with matching hats of water-repellent fabrics that had colorful printed patterns in 1958. For a commission from the fashion house Grieder he designed a mink coat in 1952, and this exclusive piece benefited from his sense of glamour.

Hubert's ideas about textile design are also revealed by a collection of fine printed-cotton fabric items that the collector Rolf Ramseier assembled in the United States. It comprised foulards and handkerchiefs, some of them with identical patterns in different colors. They show Hubert's creativity when dealing with ornaments; there are some flower motifs in addition to abstract patterns. These textiles provide an impression of the fabrics Hubert designed and his eye for decorative accessories.

Hats

As a costume designer Hubert was less interested in individual articles of clothing than the overall look. In 1927 he formulated "ten commandments for the well-dressed lady." His suggestions were distributed through a US press agency and appeared in many different languages.[20] One of them emphasized the value of accessories: "It's better to have one or two dresses that harmonize with the hat, shoes and handbag than a full closet with none of the little things that make a modern woman and demonstrate good grooming and care."[21]

Hats represented a special focus for Hubert. He created them for Marlene Dietrich, and they were also extremely significant as elements of dresses for the 1939 National Exhibition and the film costumes for Ingrid Bergman in *The Visit*. In his memoirs Hubert related numerous tales about hats, such as one decorated with flowers that Gloria Swanson wore at the funeral of Ernst Lubitsch, which was inadvertently placed on the grave as a bouquet.[22] Or how he, when at a horse race in Longchamp, desperately searched for "a hat with paradise" for his sister Rösli, a hat decorated with the feathers of a bird of paradise, which was apparently a must-have in 1939.[23] In 1947 he was even involved in the establishment of a millinery in London.[24] For the newspaper *Neue Zürcher Zeitung* he reported on London fashion

Foulard with René Hubert's imprinted signature for US company Glentex, 1950s

Mink coat for fashion boutique Grieder, Zurich, 1952

in 1938. His readers accompanied him to lunch at Claridge's, and he sketched, in both a literal and figurative sense, small portraits of society women and their hats.[25]

Hubert proved to be an excellent observer and designer of an accessory that, while no longer worn, had considerable influence on a woman's appearance together with her coiffure, jewelry and makeup in its day.

Fashion!

In the 1956 almanac of the city of St. Gallen, Hubert postulated, "'Fashion!' This rousing word that incorporates in its seven letters an entire scale of expressions and impressions! What isn't termed 'fashion!' today?! 'Fashion!' is no longer fashion alone, everything intended to be fashionable is fashion. There are fashionable conversations that follow fashionable ideas. Fashionable music that tries to fashionably seduce us, ideas that are so new we can classify them only under the word fashion. Newsstands are full of the latest fashion magazines. Fashion photos featuring the latest fashionable faces show us the latest fashions!"[26]

Hubert not only held this wide-ranging view of fashion, but he also put it into practice as a many-faceted designer. In addition to costumes he designed interiors, fabrics, dresses, hats, foulards, handkerchiefs and a great deal more. It served him well that he was literally a man of the world and at home in Paris, Berlin, London, New York and Hollywood. He had a unique sense of the zeitgeist and made his name as a luminary in his field. This was recognized and appreciated in Switzerland, his homeland, and in return he provided a link to world fashion.

1 E.g. a design by Hubert for seven-year-old Hollywood star Shirley Temple in *Curly Top* (1935).
2 Tobias Wyss, *Film heute,* portrait of René Hubert, Schweizer Fernsehen, 1975, https://www.youtube.com/watch?v=6RVexVCv8sw.
3 Marlene Dietrich, undated letter, estate of René Hubert, Cinémathèque suisse, Lausanne.
4 See the illustrations in Roland Fischer-Briand's contribution in this book, p. 131.
5 "Otto vestiti per Ingrid che torna," *Epoca* (October 10, 1963), pp. 96–103.
6 "René Hubert: Ein Schweizer – Modekönig von Hollywood," *Film-Mode,* no. 1 (1941).
7 "Der erfolgreiche René Hubert," *Film-Mode,* no. 1 (1947).
8 André R. Maugé, "Les robes de René Hubert," *Pour Vous,* July 7, 1932.
9 René Hubert, unpublished memoirs.
10 E. Hs., "Von Huber zu Hubert," *Neue Zürcher Zeitung,* May 23, 1937, p. 6.
11 Hubert, unpublished memoirs.
12 Ibid.
13 Anna-Brigitte Schlittler, "Enter the Shoe," in *Bally: A History of Footwear in the Interwar Period,* ed. Anna-Brigitte Schlittler and Katharina Tietze, Transkript, 2021, p. 111.
14 Hubert, unpublished memoirs.
15 "René Hubert entwirft Stoffe für Paris, New York, Hollywood," *Film-Mode,* no. 2 (1950).
16 https://hls-dhs-dss.ch/de/articles/031139/2012-05-29 (accessed January 1, 2022).
17 "René Hubert entwirft Stoffe."
18 Helene F. Miller, "Brief aus Los Angeles: Porträt einer Dame," *Schweizer Textilien,* no. 1 (1954), p. 79.
19 *Neue Zürcher Zeitung,* April 12, 1955. This is presumably the collection designed for the event in St. Gallen.
20 *The Evening News,* March 10, 1927; *Allgemeine Zeitung,* April 2, 1927.
21 René Hubert, "Zehn Gebote für die gut gekleidete Dame," *Die Berner Woche in Wort und Bild,* no. 21 (1927).
22 Hubert, unpublished memoirs.
23 Ibid.
24 Ibid.
25 René Hubert, "Moderennen beim Lunch," *Neue Zürcher Zeitung,* April 3, 1938.
26 René Hubert, "St. Gallen und die Mode," in *Gallus-Stadt: Jahrbuch der Stadt St. Gallen,* St. Gallen, 1956, p. 90.

Fabrics and Dresses

Textile company Stoffel & Cie, St. Gallen
pp. 189–191: dresses of piqué and other cotton fabrics designed by René Hubert, 1955

Magazine *Film-Mode* no. 2 (1950)
pp. 192–197: "René Hubert entwirft Stoffe für Paris, New York, Hollywood" ("René Hubert designs fabrics for Paris, New York, Hollywood")

***The Visit* (1964), Oscar nomination for Best Costume Design in a black-and-white film**
pp. 198–205: "Otto vestiti per Ingrid che torna" ("Eight Dresses for Ingrid's Film"), prerelease article in magazine *Epoca* (October 27, 1963), costumes by René Hubert with Nina Ricci, jewelry by Bulgari, photograph by Fortunato Scrimali

PECTOCHEWING
The New York
France-soir
N° 459
une Semaine
PAGE 2 : La bombe "H" met-elle la planète en danger?
Le procès la radio
SAMEDI-S
France Dimanche
ILLUSTRÉ
POUR POUVOIR ACCLAMER
ICI P
France-soir
Un chalutier

Von links nach rechts:
De gauche à droite:
Sundream «Maureen»
Iriton taffetas «Linda»
Iriton «Linda»
LINDA DARNELL + RENÉ HUBERT
Von links nach rechts:
De gauche à droite:
Piqué «Gene»
Piqué «Jeane»
Sundream «Betty»

nser berühmter Landsmann, der inter-
ationale Modeschöpfer René Hubert, hat
nen neuen, vorgezeichneten Weg einge-
:hlagen. Aus dem Entwerfen von Kostümen
ıd Moden für grosse Filme und elegante
ollektionen der USA kam das Verlangen,
elbst einmal Stoffe zu kreieren, die ja der
nfangspunkt jeglicher Kreationen sind.
enn der Stoff ist es, der den Entwurf und
amit die Mode bestimmt. So schafft nun
ené Hubert für das weltbekannte Haus
toffel und Co., St. Gallen, Neuheiten in
chweizer Cottonstoffen, von denen einige
ntwürfe auf der gegenüberliegenden Seite
ogebildet sind. Die erste, von dem Künst-
r signierte Kollektion hat bereits in Paris,
ew York und Hollywood einen enormen
rfolg geerntet. Seine Stoffe sind in Paris
on Dior, Balmain, Molyneux, Balenciaga,
ean Desses, Jacques Fath, Marcel Rochas,
anvin usw., mit Begeisterung in fabelhafte
leider verarbeitet worden. Die Piquémode,
e sich diesen Frühling und Sommer so
rfolgreich einzuführen und behaupten
usste, ist auf die neuen Piqués, welche
ené Hubert für Stoffel entworfen hat, zu-
ückzuführen. Für den Sommer 1951, so
rophezeit Hubert, wird eine neue Organdy-
ode einsetzen, die heute schon in herr-
chen Skizzen und neuen Geweben in den
abriken von Stoffel geboren und nächstes
ahr als René-Hubert-Schmetterlinge die
Velt erobern werden. Ein neuer Kreations-
oment für unsere Textilindustrie hat einge-
etzt, und der Verlust Hollywoods – wo René
ubert nur noch zwei Filme im Jahr machen
ird – ist hier Gewinn. Der Künstler, wel-
her in New York sein Atelier besitzt, wird
un oft in der Schweiz weilen und mithel-
n, den guten Ruf unserer Mode- und Tex-
lindustrien auszubauen und zu verbreiten.

otre éminent concitoyen René Hubert,
éateur de mode de renommée mondiale,
t l'initiateur d'une innovation très inté-
ssante. A diverses reprise déjà, le vœu
vait été émis de confectionner des étoffes
s'inspirant des projets de costumes e de
ode pour les grands films et élégantes
llections des Etat -Unis. On sait que le
ssu est le point de départ de toute création
ouvelle. C'est lui qui détermine et la coupe
la mode. René Hubert a donc lancé des
ouveautés en cotonnes d'origine suisse
our la célèbre maison Stoffel & Cie, de
aint-Gall. Vous trouverez à la page ci-
ntre quelques-uns de se· projets. La pre-
ière collection signée de cet artiste a déjà
mporté un succès énorme à Paris, à New-
ork et à Hollywood. A Paris, Dior, Bal-
ain, Molyneux, Balenciaga, Jean Desses,
acques Fath, Marcel Rochas, Lanvin, et
autres encore, ont confectionné avec en-
ousiasme, avec les étoffes de René Hubert,
es robes de toute beauté. Le tissu de piqué,
ui a réapparu et s'est imposé ce printemps
cet été, est en réalité issu des nouveaux
qués créés pour Stoffel par René Hubert.
our l'été 1951, René Hubert prédit une
ouvelle mode d'organdi, déjà née aujour-
hui dans les ravissantes esquisses et les
ouveaux tissus sortis des fabriques Stof-
l & Cie qui conquerront le monde l'année
rochaine sous le nom de «papillons» de
ené Hubert. Notre industrie textile s'est
nsi enrichie d'un nouvel élément créateur
la perte ressentie à Hollywood – où
ené Hubert ne tournera plus que deux film,
r an – est pour la Suisse une aubaine·
artiste, dont l'atelier se trouve à New-
ork, séjournera désormais fréquemment
Suisse et contribuera à répandre et à
re mieux connaître le bon renom de nos
dustries suisses du textile et de la mode.

René Hubert

entwirft Stoffe für Paris, New York, Hollywood

Robe en piqué nouveauté, façonné rose et noir.

Robe manteau en piqué nouveauté bleu à pois noirs.

René Hubert

crée des tissus pour Paris, New-York, Hollywood

Bluse aus rosa Piqué mit schwarzen Punkten; Kragen und Manschetten aus schwarzem Samt.

Blouse en piqué rose à pois noirs, col et manchettes en velours noir.

Hut und Kragen aus weissem Piqué.
Chapeaux et col en piqué blanc.

Piqué
Chemisier aus gestreiftem Piqué in gelb oder schwarz.
Chemisier en piqué quadrillé de couleur jaune ou noir.
Blaues Piquékleid mit gelben Punkten auf blauem Grund. Grosse Revers aus weissem Piqué.
Robe en piqué sur fond bleu, pois jaunes. – Grand revers en piqué blanc.
RH

Tailleur aus Twill imprimé mit Mousselinebluse.
Tailleur en twill imprimé avec blouse de mousseline.
Bluse aus gestreiftem Twill zu uni Jupe.
Twill tissé quadrillé avec jupe unie.
Bot.

Twill

Kleid aus buntem Twill mit uni Bolero.

Robe en twill imprimé, jupe plissée.

Robe de twill rose imprimé de dessin marron. Ceinture de cuir.

Otto vestiti per Ingrid che torna

Ingrid Bergman ritorna. A quarantasei anni la famosa attrice svedese, che sostituì nell'immaginazione del pubblico del dopoguerra i personaggi, diventati mitici, di Greta Garbo e Marlene Dietrich, raffigura ancora l'incanto, la classe, la dolcezza, lo stile della vecchia Europa. In queste pagine e in quelle che seguono la Bergman è ritratta con otto abiti da lei indossati nel film « La vendetta della signora », che si sta girando a Roma ed è stato tratto da un dramma dello scrittore svizzero Friedrich Dürrenmatt. Dalle pagine acri e spietate di Dürrenmatt balza, come per prodigio, questo favoloso « ritratto di signora », immerso in un alone di eleganza quasi irreale.

Foto di Fortunato Scrimali

*A sinistra:
un abito di pizzo bianco con fili d'argento. È un modello di Hubert, confezionato da Nina Ricci. Gioielli di Bulgari: collier di diamanti, un solitario al dito. La Bergman, nel film, indossa quest'abito quando i compaesani la festeggiano, al suo ritorno. Lei, ricchissima, promette loro due milioni di dollari se uccideranno il suo ex innamorato.*

*A destra:
un'immagine misteriosa e suggestiva dell'attrice, che qui simboleggia la Vendetta. Quest'abito nero con un mantello adorno di una volpe e un gran cappello pure nero, di stile romantico, viene indossato da Ingrid quando lascia il paese, alla fine del film. Il dramma di Dürrenmatt, da cui il film è tratto, fu scritto nel 1956.*

Questa tuta superba laminata in oro, con spolverino verde giada (un'altra creazione di Nina Ricci), trasforma Ingrid Bergman in una ieratica figura egizia. Il film narra una storia senza pietà: Karla (la Bergman) è stata delusa, anni prima, nel suo amore per Miller (Anthony Quinn). Divenuta potente, complotta per farlo uccidere.

Un altro modello esotico: Nina Ricci, mentre lo creava, s'è ispirata al Giappone. Si chiama Butterfly *e ricorda il teatro Kabuki. Sul fondo bianco ghiaccio sono stampati fiori blu, tabacco, celeste, arancione e verde prato. Il valore degli smeraldi e brillanti rari che l'attrice porta durante le scene del film ammonta a 400 milioni.*

A sinistra:
un abito
quasi evanescente
per una scena
d'amore:
è di vetro filato
celeste,
orlato di raso
e composto
di una tunica
con mantella
sovrapposta,
dello stesso tessuto,
ispirato
ai ponchos messicani
(creazione
di Nina Ricci).
Accanto alla Bergman
recitano
Anthony Quinn, Stoppa,
Valentina Cortese,
Romolo Valli
e Irina Demich.

A destra:
una donna stupenda
quanto crudele
passeggia
nella piazza
del paese
che ha atterrito.
Ha una tunica
di shantung,
mantello a ruota
di chiffon,
e sa celare
i guizzi maliziosi
del viso
con un ombrellino
che ne esaspera
la civetteria.
La ricca parure
sfavilla
di smeraldi purissimi.
Il volto
di questa Vendetta
appare irresistibile.

100

*Un abito tigrato,
con striature brune
dipinte a mano.
Il tessuto,
come tutti gli altri,
è esclusivo
e apparirà
nelle collezioni
parigine
di primavera.
Nella scena
in cui lo indossa
la protagonista,
severa
come una dea greca,
sta per ricevere
l'antico innamorato,
il quale è convinto
che la caccia
orribile
scatenata dalla donna
contro di lui
sia tutta uno scherzo.*

*L'implacabile Karla,
mentre ascolta musiche di Brahms,
indossa questo completo con pantaloni in oro
e redingote in broccato,
ispirato al costume nazionale indiano.
La Bergman, di cui presentiamo questi ritratti
in esclusiva mondiale, ha sbalordito
il regista Bernhard Wicki, che è stato costretto
a « invecchiarla » perché l'attrice dimostra
meno dei trentotto anni del suo personaggio.*

“Swissair planes have two things in common with Hollywood’s leading filmstars – both move on an exalted level and both are dressed by the same man. His name is René Hubert.... Seven hours from the sky-scrapers to the Alps with champagne, caviar and a Marlene Dietrich setting. Who said there’s no romance in this twentieth century?”

Charlotte Peter, 1960

Taking Off into the Jet Age: Corporate Design for Swissair

Andres Janser

Whoever flew Swissair in the 1950s or 1960s was surrounded by René Hubert's work. He designed both the textiles used in all jets' interiors and the stewardesses' uniforms. Not only were all textiles created by a single individual, this was done by a renowned Hollywood costume designer and fashion designer – which was unheard of in civilian aviation at the time.

Hubert's entry into this new field was facilitated by a more profound change. Pressured by US airlines, the International Air Transport Association introduced a new class with less-expensive fares in 1952. At the same time aircraft manufacturers were producing increasingly large propeller-driven planes that required fewer layovers. All in all, these changes enabled a marked increase in volume, including in overseas air traffic, as flying was now negligibly more expensive than surface travel and several days shorter. By 1957 the numbers of air and ship passengers on the North Atlantic route were equal, with one million each.[1] Civilian use of jetliners was also on the horizon, which meant even shorter traveling times, greater distances and space for more passengers.

For Swissair, which had a small domestic market, international customers were especially important. A new CEO joined the company in 1950 and was successful with his speculative policy of expansion, on the route between Europe and North America at first and soon after to South America, Asia and Africa. Swissair also became a trendsetter in terms of cultivating its image.[2] Before the war the company had already hired excellent graphic designers who worked on its visual identity. Starting in 1952 this was dominated by Rudolf Bircher's design, with the sprawling lettering and the flying arrow logo, which anticipated the jet age with its swept-back wings ("Swissair arrow").[3]

Swissair had already taken the first step toward establishing a corporate design two years previously when it hired Hubert. This was the company's reaction to the growing competition, some of which flew the same long routes. As Swissair CEO Walter Berchtold put it years later, its business strategy of hiring a "fashion designer who was familiar with America" to create the airline's textiles made this move an obvious choice.[4] Robert Fretz, a captain at Swissair since 1938 and an advocate of expanding the intercontinental traffic who flew the North Atlantic route regularly, brought up the name René Hubert.[5] Originally trained as a painter, Fretz personified the combination of culturally well-grounded Americanism and economic sense.[6]

A broad methodical basis for the concept of corporate design did not yet exist, and there had been little trial of one for service companies like airlines. In Hubert's work, which was not in the advertising department responsible for visual appearance, aircraft development seemed to drive his design: the appearance of new aircraft models, which happened every few years, projected an image of progress that was amplified in new uniform collections.

From the Cabin to the Uniform

In summer 1951 Swissair received its first two DC-6B long-range propeller-driven aircraft, which had been ordered one year previously. This meant Hubert was presumably hired for cabin textiles and colors in late 1950. He designed the seat covers, walls and ceilings in light shades of gray.[7] The side panels of the seats – the shape of which was determined by the manufacturer and was the same for all airlines they supplied – were dark blue, and both the armrests and carpets were dark red, producing striking color highlights. As a result the planes, which offered few opportunities for design overall, being mass-produced, were given an appearance specific to Swissair.

When the third DC-6B was delivered in late 1952, passengers could choose between two classes, the existing standard class (now first class) and the newly introduced tourist class (later called economy). Hubert's basic design apparently remained in use later with the next model, the Douglas DC-7C (Seven Seas) and the medium-range Convair CV-440.

In 1934 Swissair was the first European airline to employ a female stewardess in addition to male stewards. In larger planes the intention was to outdo the competition with the food served on board. As a result, the stewardesses – as the main hostesses who greeted passengers – became part of the marketing, in which fashion also played an important role.[8] The military look of their uniforms, which was common at many airlines,[9] would be dispensed with

Tourist class in Douglas DC-6, first used in 1951

First class in Convair CV-440 Metropolitan, first used in 1956

and the new outfits worn consistently, which apparently was not always the case: "Our stewardesses look like members of the Women's Army Auxiliary Corps,[10] in other words too military. Furthermore, their clothing is not uniform (shoes!). A new uniform should be worn by all flight attendants. In addition, a summer uniform is needed. (Dr. Berchtold passed around a few of Hubert's drawings with ideas of what a new stewardess uniform could look like: gray tailored suit, red pockets and shoes; in other words, the same colors as the interiors of our new DC-6Bs)."[11]

The grays and reds in the aircraft's cabins therefore served as a guideline for a uniform overall appearance. The waisted jacket had cuffs on its sleeves, and there was a matching white blouse, a hat that resembled a beret and a long skirt. Light-gray aprons were worn for on-board service.

Into the Golden Age with Jets

The actual golden age began for Swissair with jets. In 1960 long-haul Douglas DC-8s were put in service. While the first DC-6Bs had been limited to 54 seats, the new flagship was designed for 130 passengers, three-fourths of them in economy class.

The cabin was a large, open space with 24 rows, and Hubert worked on the interior design in a manufacturer's mock-up in Long Beach, California, in 1958. After the seats were patterned with a variety of colors, the established trio was kept with unpatterned fabrics, which he gave a striking new look: sky blue, white and the bright red of the Swiss flag, which was already used in the logo. For an article in *Swissair-Gazette* he summarized his convincingly modernized concept in words fit for a screenplay: "The passenger must get an impression of lightness. As soon as he boards a plane, he must feel airborne. For that reason only the colors of the sky suit jet planes: the cottony white of the clouds and the lustrous blue of the distant horizon. In other words, the cabin becomes a fragment of a stylized sky."[12]

Design is created in a dialogue with clients and manufacturers. When answering the question about how decisions were made, their consistent implementation over time is also important in the case of corporate design. Swissair was apparently not immune to the difficulties involved: in the carefully designed brochure to announce the launch of the DC-8, reference to the country, important for cultivating the company's image, was made in curtains

Europe's first stewardess, Nelly Diener, 1934

Flight attendants in a 1952 uniform in front of a Douglas DC-6

Flight attendant in a 1958 uniform

Swissair Uniformen-Reglement, 1956, summer uniform (top) and winter uniform (bottom)

Hostess

Sommeruniform

Beret, Jacke, Bluse (offener Kragen), weisse Handschuhe, geschlossene Pumps

Hostess

Winteruniform

Beret, Halstuch, Mantel, dunkelblaue Handschuhe, Winterstiefel

René Hubert working on interior of DC-8, 1958

Seat patterns in a Douglas aircraft mock-up in Long Beach

Meeting at the studio of Douglas Aircraft

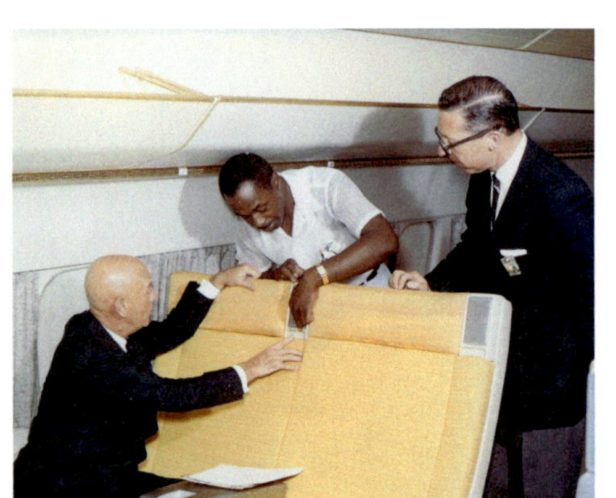

Swissair training mock-up at Zurich Airport, 1960

Clockwise from top left:
First-class lounge

First class

Tourist class

Tourist-class cabin, *Schweizer Filmwochenschau,* film frame

with elegant stripes in Switzerland's colors, red and white[13] > pp. 230-231. When mass-produced, these curtains were then apparently printed with stylized "Swiss Alpine flowers,"[14] which harmonized with the bright sunflower yellow, light blue and ruby red of floor coverings, headrests and napkins.

For this new generation of aircraft Hubert updated his original uniform collection in 1958: the hems of both the jacket and the skirt were noticeably higher, and the blouse was now worn open. Without lapels, the jackets seemed more minimal, while the winter coat was given a striking shawl collar.

Final Designs

The order of twelve Douglas DC-9s for short and medium routes was the occasion for a new collection in 1965, which would be Hubert's final work. Three dozen sketches survive, and they reveal the great pleasure that someone who was then at the age of seventy had designing > pp. 221-29. As customary he spent a great deal of effort on the hats and – presumably without being asked – a fur cap for winter. One reason for the numerous variations was the fact that the stewardesses had obtained a say in the process.

A change in the basic color was apparently as out of the question as were printed fabrics. As a result, he dispensed with the watercolor drawings he made to depict his opulent camera-oriented costume designs – most recently those in 1963 for Ingrid Bergman in *The Visit* – and highlighted his conceptual ideas more powerfully with the bold strokes of a felt-tip pen.

The most conspicuous element of the mostly newly conceived uniform was the light-blue blouse with a stand-up collar. It was tailored of wrinkle-free nylon, which made washing it en route easier. That was also the case with the new tropical dress, which became necessary after a successful expansion of the routes. In windy weather a light chiffon scarf held the hat in place while the wearer walked across the apron.

Hollywood and Corporate Design

Hubert's work for Swissair was lucrative, as it covered a more than twenty-piece collection with summer and winter elements. The cabin design scheme was soon expanded to encompass blankets, pillowcases, napkins and tablecloths. As a result, his expertise designing visual presences as a whole paid off

1958 uniform

Flight attendant with felt hat

Flight attendants in summer uniform (top) and winter uniform (bottom)

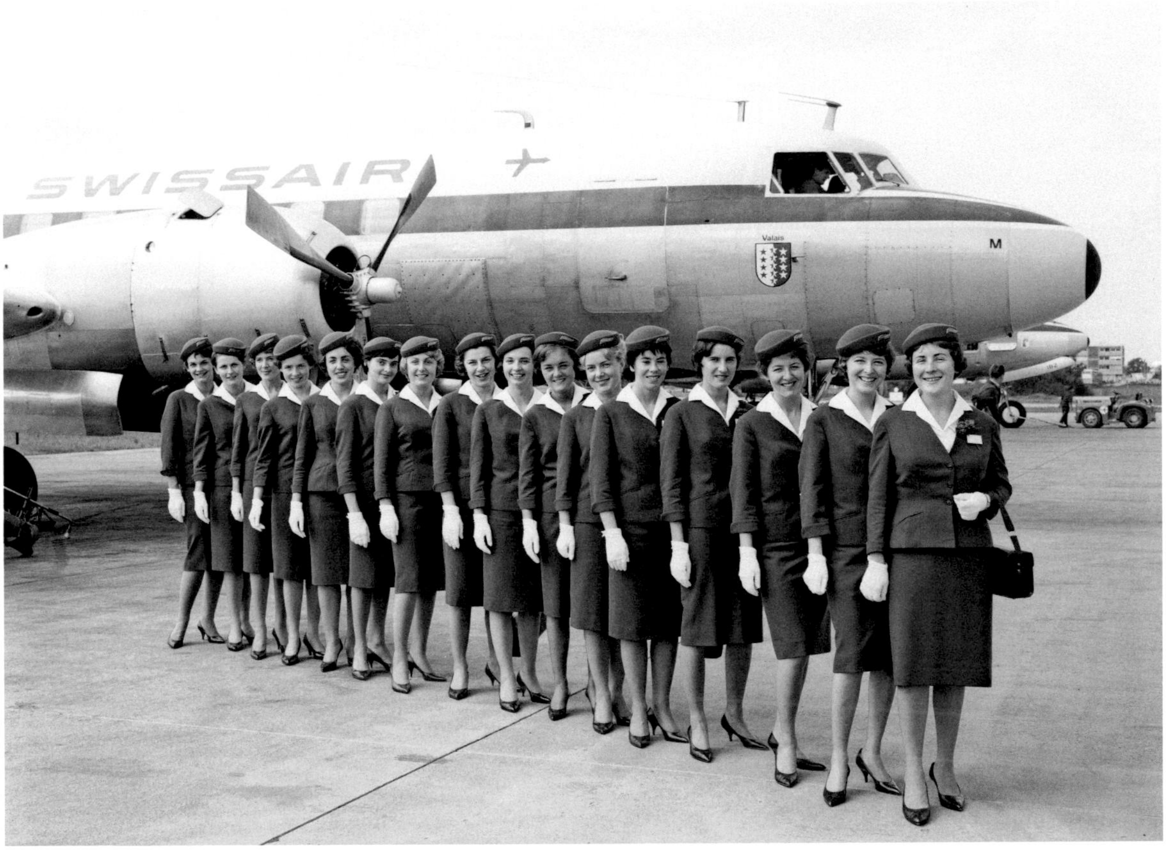
SWISSAIR
Valais
M

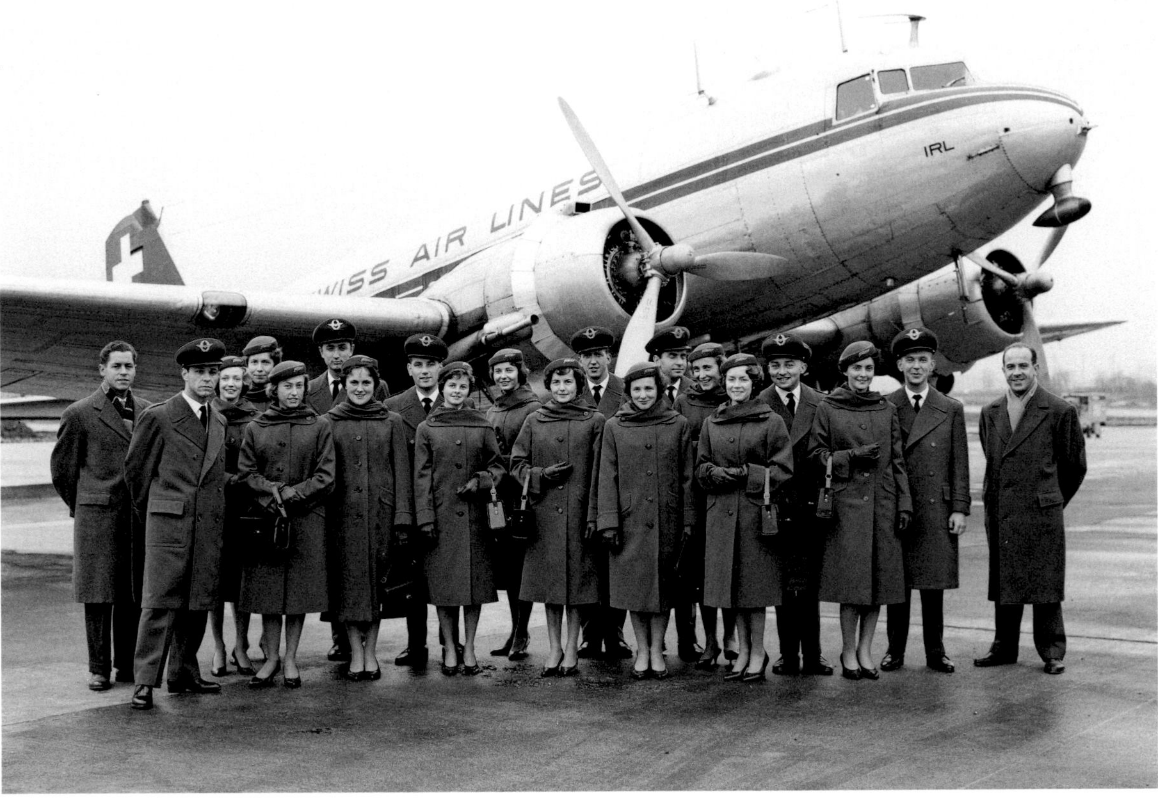
SWISS AIR LINES
IRL

>pp. 230-31. At the same time, he had no reason to suspect that Swissair would be successful in the long term or what importance it would place on continuity: in the end the company relied on him for nearly twenty years[15] – in contrast to other airlines, which worked with a different fashion house for every new uniform collection. This presumably made Hubert's life in Switzerland easier.

After saying goodbye to Hollywood to an extent, Hubert took a similar path as Howard Greer, who was the same age. The latter designed costumes for Irene Dunne and Katharine Hepburn while establishing himself as a couturier. His uniforms for Transcontinental & Western Air (TWA) in 1944 made him the first designer for an airline with a background in film. Other companies made use of the glamour of Hollywood designers: in 1958 Pan American World Airways (Pan Am) hired Don Loper, who had just created clothing for Marlene Dietrich, and ten years later United Air Lines employed Jean Louis, the former head costume designer at Columbia Pictures.[16]

Hubert was able to unite fashion expertise and Hollywood glamour with the airline's self-image of professionalism.[17] Thanks to his designs the former uniforms' military look was quickly forgotten and the consistent smoky blue shade became a trademark as "Swissair blue." His collections satisfied Swissair's expectations to such a great extent that the uniforms were also used in advertisements. Management reiterated its rejection of anything that was too fashionable: "The example set by the Swiss was soon imitated, and a true fashion competition developed among the airlines, though one in which Swissair did not participate."[18] However, Hubert's work represents a successful combination of modernity, for which aviation was paradigmatic, and a profound sense of fashion. This was on his part a remarkable contribution to the jet age and its aesthetic.[19]

Flying became increasingly affordable in the years Hubert – himself a frequent flier due to his work obligations – helped shape the image of Swissair without it becoming too normal. Swissair saw itself in the upmarket segment, and Hubert helped the company create the desired ambiance for all those who could afford and wished to partake in "flying as part of a glamorous and romantic life."[20] In the words of the travel writer Charlotte Peter in the abovementioned article for *Swissair-Gazette* accompanying a "star portrait" of Hubert: "Swissair planes

1966 uniform

Summer and winter uniforms at photo studio

Flight attendant on the runway at Zurich Airport

Summer uniform and tropical dress in DC-8 training mock-up

have two things in common with Hollywood's leading filmstars – both move on an exalted level and both are dressed by the same man. His name is René Hubert.... Seven hours from the sky-scrapers to the Alps with champagne, caviar and a Marlene Dietrich setting. Who said there's no romance in this twentieth century?"[21]

Portrait of René Hubert for *Swissair-Gazette* (1960), photograph by © Michael Wolgensinger/Fotostiftung Schweiz

1 Alfred Waldis, "Aufstieg und Niedergang der Nordatlantikschifffahrt," *Neue Zürcher Zeitung*, April 29, 1989, pp. 86–88.
2 Possibly inspired by the work of FHK Henrion for the British Overseas Airways Corporation (BOAC) in the years after the war ended. See Jochen Eisenbrand, "Fluggesellschaften und Corporate Design," in *Airworld: Design und Architektur für die Flugreise*, ed. Jochen Eisenbrand and Alexander von Vegesack, Weil am Rhein, 2004, pp. 144–174.
3 In contrast the wings of prop planes are nearly perpendicular.
4 Walter Berchtold, *Durch Turbulenzen zum Erfolg: 22 Jahre am Steuer der Swissair*, Zurich, 1981, p. 112.
5 Ibid.
6 In his autobiography Robert Fretz went into detail concerning Hubert's work without mentioning that he was the one to involve him. See Robert Fretz, *Swissair im Kampf und Aufstieg: Ein autobiographischer Beitrag zur Geschichte der Swissair*, Zurich, 1973.
7 Shades of gray had already been used for Bally locations. See Katharina Tietze's contribution in this book.
8 Pilots and stewards normally continued to wear off-the-shelf uniforms that were inspired by sailor suits. See Joanne Entwistle, "Mode auf dem Höhenflug: Die Flugbegleiterin und ihre Uniform," in *Airworld: Design und Architektur für die Flugreise*, ed. Jochen Eisenbrand and Alexander von Vegesack, Weil am Rhein, 2004, pp. 176–210.
9 Air France also hired Georgette de Trèze in 1951 to create a collection of fashionable uniforms, which were then adopted in 1954.
10 The Women's Army Auxiliary Corps was established in 1939 as part of the Swiss army.
11 Swissair Board of Directors, meeting minutes, June 14, 1951, Verkehrshaus der Schweiz, VA/L-20110223.04. The uniform in use was already a subdued grayish blue in 1946.
12 Charlotte Peter, "René Hubert: The Man Who Dresses Filmstars and Aircraft," *Swissair Gazette*, no. 3 (March 1960), p. 13.
13 The photographs were taken in the training mock-up that Swissair had made.
14 Peter, "René Hubert," p. 13.
15 His last collection was replaced by Julia Diethelm's in 1970. See Wolfgang Schmittel, "Swissair," in *Design Concept Realisation*, ed. Wolfgang Schmittel, Zurich, 1975, pp. 197–224. Karl Gerster's concept for graphic design replaced that of Rudolf Bircher in 1981.
16 The path from film to planes could also take place in reverse: stewardesses at Alitalia, which was founded after the war, wore uniforms from the fashion boutique Sorelle Fontana. After the three sisters created a dress for the actor Linda Christian's 1949 wedding with Hollywood star Tyrone Power, film stars such as Audrey Hepburn, Grace Kelly and Elizabeth Taylor became its clients.
17 Combining fashion and a serious image for the world of travel was also desired for a subsequent 1959 commission from Bern's Hotel Schweizerhof. For its 100th anniversary Hubert designed new uniforms for its personnel. See "Le Schweizerhof à Berne, un alerte et pimpant centenaire," *Hotel-Revue*, April 16, 1959, p. 25.
18 Berchtold, *Turbulenzen*, p. 119.
19 For a broad outline of the aesthetics of the jet age, see Vanessa R. Schwartz, *Jet Age Aesthetic: The Glamour of Media in Motion*, New Haven, 2020.
20 Entwistle, "Mode auf dem Höhenflug," p. 177.
21 Peter, "René Hubert," p. 12.

Advertising posters for Swissair, layout by Jakob Tobler, photograph by Achille Wieder

Left: Flight attendant in 1958 uniform, 1965

Right: Flight attendant in 1966 uniform, 1967

1958 and 1966 uniforms, exhibition *René Hubert – Kleider machen Stars*, Museum für Gestaltung Zürich, 2021

Final Designs

Swissair flight-attendant uniforms
pp. 221–229: designs, 1965, for flight-attendants of Swissair's Douglas DC-9

Swissair Douglas DC-8
pp. 230/231: folder for initial service, layout by Max Schneider, 1960

SEPARATE
ECHÂRPE
AUS
GLEICHEM
STOFF.
KNÖPFF
METALL

7
Diese
Mantel hatte
38 Punkte
also in diesem
Genre etwas!

1

Dieses ist ausgewählt worden!

35
36
37

27
28
29

Knöpfe
Tropen Kleid

VESTE UBER BLUSE GETRAGEN
VESTE KANN AUCH HÖHER GESCHLOSSEN SEIN.

TROPENKLEID

55
56
FOR WINTER!
57
BLAK FUR HATS.

JUMPER KLEID + JACKE
KANN OHNE BLUSE GETRAGEN WERDEN.

46
47
48
49

BORD DU CHAPEAU VERNIS NOIR
CEINTURE VERNIS NOIR
WEISSE BLUSE MIT GURTEL VORNE

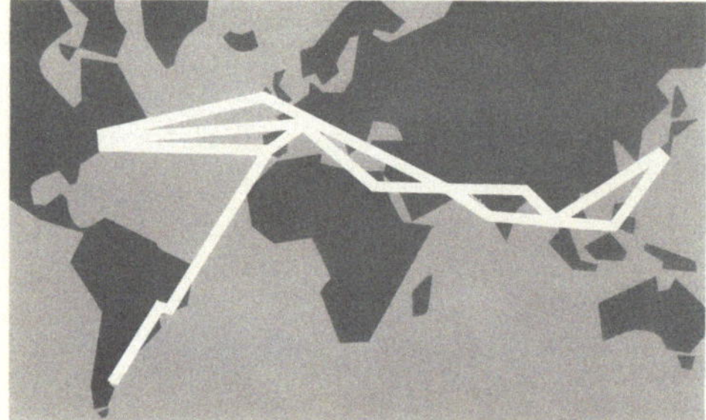

Ob Ihr Reiseziel in Nord- oder Südamerika, in Europa, im Nahen oder Fernen Osten liegt, Swissair bietet Ihnen mit ihrem gutausgebauten Streckennetz immer schnelle und komfortable Reisemöglichkeiten.

Zwischen Europa und den Vereinigten Staaten verkürzen Douglas DC-8 Strahlflugzeuge die Reisezeiten bedeutend. In Europa und im Mittleren Osten fliegen mit Rolls-Royce-Strahltriebwerken ausgerüstete Caravelles. Ab Mitte 1961 gelangen über dem Südatlantik, zwischen Europa und Südamerika, sowie auf den Strecken von Europa nach dem Fernen Osten Strahlflugzeuge vom Typ Convair 600 «Coronado» in den Verkehr.

Ihnen Ihre Reisen so angenehm wie möglich zu gestalten, betrachtet das Personal der Swissair als seine schönste und grösste Aufgabe. Überall, zu Lande und in der Luft, werden Sie vom freundlichen Personal nicht einfach als irgendein Passagier, sondern als willkommener, lieber Gast empfangen und allen Ihren Wünschen wird immer persönliche Aufmerksamkeit geschenkt. Ob Sie mit der Swissair auf einer kurzen oder langen Strecke, in einem Kolbenmotor- oder Strahlflugzeug fliegen, etwas ist immer genau gleich: der hohe Standard des Swissair-Service.

Ihr Reisebüro wird Ihnen bestätigen: Flugpreise sind alle gleich; der Unterschied liegt im Service. Fliegen Sie mit der Swissair — weltweit.

Gastfreundschaft

Als exklusive Swissair-Neuheit erhält jeder Fluggast der Ersten Klasse seine ganz individuelle, nach seinen eigenen Wünschen und persönlichen Anregungen zusammengesetzte Feinschmecker-Mahlzeit.

Das ist nur möglich, weil Sie schon beim Bestellen des Flugscheines eine riesige Menukarte mit einer bis anhin noch nie auf einem Flugzeug offerierten, unglaublichen Auswahl der herrlichsten Leckerbissen erhalten. Zu Hause, in aller Ruhe, können Sie Ihre Mahlzeit zusammenstellen, Ihre Wünsche auf einer vorgedruckten Karte notieren und Ihre Bestellung an die guten Geister der Swissair-Traumküche senden.

Mit viel Liebe, Sorgfalt und meisterhaftem Können bereiten sodann die Swissair-Küchenchefs jedem einzelnen Fluggast die gewünschten Herrlichkeiten zu. Jedem Detail — sei es auch noch so winzig klein — wird grosse Beachtung geschenkt. Selbstverständlich werden auch Diätvorschriften gewissenhaft eingehalten.

Ein zufriedenes, geniesserisches Lächeln strahlt über das Gesicht eines jeden Fluggastes, wenn die charmante Hostess nach dem Apéritif die kulinarischen Meisterwerke serviert. Selbst wenn Sie sich erst im allerletzten Moment zu dem Flug entschliessen, kommen die findigen Swissair-Chefs noch lange nicht in Verlegenheit. Für diese Fälle halten sie stets eine Auswahl der beliebtesten Menus bereit.

Komfort

Kabine der Economy-Class

Die Douglas DC-8 bietet aber nicht nur den Fluggästen allen erdenklichen Komfort; sie verfügt auch über grosse, zweckmässig eingerichtete Frachträume. Jede einzelne Sendung wird durch das geschulte Frachtpersonal sorgfältig behandelt. Für grosse und schwere Sendungen stehen dem Bodendienst modernste Verlademittel zur Verfügung.

Mit Luftfracht gewinnen Sie Zeit und sparen an Verpackungskosten und Versicherungsprämien. Ihr Spediteur, oder die nächste Swissair Frachtannahmestelle, geben Ihnen gerne weitere Auskunft.

Schneider, Printed in Switzerland 60. Gebr. Fretz AG. Zürich

nosphäre der Freude strahlt das farbenfrohe der geräumigen Economy-Class-Kabine aus. Die ablen, herrlich weichen Fauteuils laden Sie zum n ein. Ein leichter Druck auf einen Knopf in der e — schon senkt sich die Rückenlehne Ihres Sitzes ten und Sie können ein erquickendes Schläfchen Es stört Sie dabei nicht im geringsten, wenn Ihr lesen will, denn die neben dem Kopfpolster eines tzes eingebaute individuelle Leselampe spendet nehm gleichmässiges, ruhiges und nur auf den nden Platz konzentriertes Licht.

e Essenszeit naht, so zieht die Hostess aus der d Ihres Vordersitzes ein praktisches Klapptischchen nd stellt Ihnen darauf ein Tablett mit einer herrlichen t vor. Guten Appetit!

s in die Rückwand Ihres Vordersitzes sind ein Frisch- en, den Sie ganz nach Ihrem eigenen Gutdünken en können, und ein Rufknopf für die Bedienung ut.

sorgt von freundlichen Hostessen, die den Wün- er Fluggäste persönliche Aufmerksamkeit schenken, einen nur das leise Rauschen des aussen vorbei- en Luftstromes daran, dass man sich auf 12 000 m it ungefähr 15 km in der Minute seinem Ziel nähert.

DC 8

Die Douglas DC-8 ist das neueste Langstreckenflugzeug der Swissair. Dieses mit vier Pratt und Whitney-Triebwerken ausgerüstete Strahlflugzeug erreicht eine maximale Geschwindigkeit von 950 km/h, das sind 15,8 km in der Minute! Die durchschnittliche Reisegeschwindigkeit der Douglas DC-8 beträgt 900 km/h, oder 15 km pro Minute.

In der Erstklass-Kabine mit ihrer gemütlichen Lounge, aber auch in der Economy-Class-Kabine — überall im Flugzeug — haben Sie ungewöhnlich viel Platz und können sich frei und ungezwungen bewegen.

Und noch etwas wird Ihnen auffallen: die angenehme, wohltuende Ruhe in der Kabine. Sie hören fast kein Motorengeräusch. Sie spüren aber auch keine Erschütterung — auf 12 000 m Höhe herrschen wenig atmosphärische Störungen. Die Triebwerke der Douglas DC-8 haben keine Kolben, die Vibrationen verursachen könnten.

All das erhöht die Freude am Reisen und macht das Fliegen mit einer DC-8 zum Genuss. Aber nicht allein die geschmackvolle Einrichtung, nicht nur der luxuriöse Komfort, sondern auch der traditionelle, vorbildliche Swissair-Service und die ausgezeichneten Swissair-Mahlzeiten lassen den DC-8 Flug zum unvergesslichen, schönen Erlebnis werden.

Geschwindigkeit

SWISSAIR

Erstklass-Kabine

First Class Lounge

1 Eintrittsöffnung
2 Kompressor
3 Brennkammern
4 Turbine
5 Düse

Die Arbeitsweise eines Strahltriebwerkes: Vorne, bei der Eintrittsöffnung saugt ein Kompressor Luft an, verdichtet sie und presst sie in die Brennkammern. Dort wird Brennstoff in die komprimierte Luft eingespritzt, das Druckluft/Brennstoff-Gemisch wird entzündet, dehnt sich aus und drängt nach hinten. Bevor jedoch die heissen Gase das Triebwerk durch die Düse verlassen können, werden sie durch eine Gasturbine geleitet. Diese Turbine und der Kompressor sind durch die gleiche Welle miteinander verbunden. Die Drehzahl des Kompressors richtet sich somit nach der Drehzahl der Turbine, die anderseits durch den Gasstrom, abhängig vom zugeführten Wärmeinhalt, beeinflusst wird. Somit entsteht im Triebwerk ein kontinuierlicher Luft-Verbrennungsgas-Strom. Nach einem Gesetz «Aktion — Reaktion» wird durch die beschleunigten ausströmenden Gase ein Schub, das heisst die Antriebskraft, durch welche das Flugzeug nach vorne geschoben wird, erzeugt.

René Hubert in supporting role in Ufa production
Hokuspokus/The Temporary Widow (1930)

René Eugen Huber

René Eugen Huber was born on October 7, 1895, in Frauenfeld, Switzerland. His father, Eugen, and mother, Rosa (née Ruckstuhl), ran a riding stable in St. Gallen. He grew up there, attended the vocational school and completed training as an embroidery designer. In 1916 he went to Paris to study painting, first at the École des Beaux-Arts and later at the private Académie Colarossi. In line with French pronunciation he added a *t* to his name and thereafter called himself René Hubert.

In 1919, Hubert made a trip to New York, Buenos Aires and Madrid. Then he worked for fashion boutiques in Paris, and starting in fall 1920 spent a year in New York, where he ran a branch of a wholesale millinery and designed his first costumes for the Shubert brothers' stages. After returning to Paris, he won a competition for stage costumes and Bénédicte Rasimi, director of the music hall Ba-ta-Clan (now Bataclan), paid him five francs (now about sixty euros) per design for new shows.

Madame Sans-Gêne with Gloria Swanson, the first film for which Hubert designed all the costumes, was his breakthrough in film in 1925. Over the subsequent ten years he worked in Hollywood for Famous Players-Lasky/Paramount, Metro-Goldwyn-Mayer and Fox Film, for Universum Film (Ufa) in Berlin and Films Sonores Tobis in Paris. From 1931 to 1933 he was a head designer for the first time, at Les Studios Paramount in Paris. He held the same position in 1935–1939 at London Films in London and in 1942–1949 at 20th Century-Fox in Hollywood. He worked with directors such as Allan Dwan, Alfred Hitchcock, Ernst Lubitsch and Otto Preminger, switched from silent to sound film and left his mark on works in both black-and-white and color. For his last film, *The Visit,* he received his second Oscar nomination in 1965.

At the same time Hubert continued designing for the stage, doing the most work in his years in London and then later in Los Angeles, New York, St. Gallen, Zurich and Geneva. In both areas he benefited from his ability to speak several languages. In order to stay on top of things with regard to fashion, he regularly traveled to Paris. There were friendships lasting many years with the actors Gloria Swanson, Marlene Dietrich, Merle Oberon and Ingrid Bergman, the director René Clair and the costume designer Charles Le Maire.

Hubert's international fame led to work in his home country. At the Swiss National Exhibition in 1939 he designed the shows in the fashion theater. After that he designed fabric and fashion collections for textile companies in St. Gallen and fashion boutiques and department stores in Zurich. In 1950–1966 he created all of Swissair's cabin interiors and uniforms for female flight attendants. In 1952 he received Swiss citizenship, having renounced it to become a US citizen in 1945.

From 1952 Hubert lived in St. Gallen, then moved to Zurich in 1960. He lived there with his partner, Georges Stamatiadis (born January 23, 1924, on the Greek island of Aegina, died May 14, 1978, in Zurich), whom he met in the 1950s. They traveled together to Brazil, Morocco, the United States and Southeast Asia. His memoirs have never been published. Hubert, who called himself a *créateur,* died on June 5, 1976, in Zurich.

Costumes for Stage Plays and Films

Andres Janser, Angelo Luerti, Rolf Ramseier

Editorial note
The works are arranged according to the date of the first performance/release date since the respective production start is often unknown. The present list of works takes into account program notes of stage productions, opening and closing credits of films and information from stage and film magazines. Around 1934, René Hubert compiled a list of all the actresses he had dressed up to that time; this document was helpful in researching films for Paramount Studios. Another list, which Hubert made in the 1960s, as well as his unpublished memoirs, led to the discovery of other previously unknown works.

D: Director
P: Production
C: Cast
R: Release/opening night
E: Explanatory note
S: Selected costumes by René Hubert
U: René Hubert uncredited, documented by source
A: Attributed to René Hubert

Stage plays

1920–1932: New York, Paris, Berlin
Kissing Time, Lyric Theatre, New York, **P:** Empire Producing Co., **D:** Edward Royce, **C:** Leslie Henson, Phyllis Dare, Stanley Holloway, **R:** 10.11.1920, **E:** S, U
June Love, Knickerbocker Theatre, New York, **P:** Sherman Brown, **D:** George Vivian, **C:** Else Adler, Bertee Beaumont, Alice Gordon, W. B. Davidson, **R:** 4.25.1921, **E:** S, U
Princess Virtue, Central Theatre, New York, **P:** Gerard F. Bacon, **D:** Leon Errol, **C:** Sarah Edwards, Hugh Cameron, Earle Foxe, Jules Epailly, **R:** 5.4.1921, **E:** S, U
Théâtre de La Chauve-Souris, Théâtre Femina, Paris, **P/D:** Nikita Balieff, **R:** 1920, **E:** S, U. The *Théâtre de La Chauve-Souris* made several guest appearances in Paris from 1920 to 1925 – it is unknown for which season Hubert designed.
De Toutes les Couleurs, Ba-ta-clan, Paris, **P:** Bénédicte Rasimi, **D:** Roger Ferréol, Georges Dolley, **C:** Cariel, C. James, H. Bandin, Galan, Edmond Guy, Lambel, Bénédicte Rasimi, **R:** 1.1922, **E:** S
Ziegfeld Follies of 1922*,* New Amsterdam Theatre, New York, **P:** Lee und J. J. Shubert, **D:** Ned Wayburn, **C:** Martha Lorber, Gilda Gray, Mary Eaton, Will Rogers, **R:** 6.5.1922, **E:** S, U
Vive la Femme!, Palace Music-Hall, Paris, **P/D:** Oscar Duffrene, Henri Varna, **C:** Maurice Chevalier, Yvonne Vallée, Rahna, Max Berger, 10.15.1924, **E:** S
An Alle, Grosses Schauspielhaus, Berlin, **P/D:** Erik Charell, **C:** John Tiller Girls, Diane Belli, Mars, Dina Gralla, **R:** 10.18.1924, **E:** S
La revue trés excitante, Concert Mayol, Paris, **P/D:** Leo Leleivre, Fernand Rouveat, Henri Varna, **C:** Dora Stroeva, Jane Aubert, Edmond Castel, **R:** 1.1.1925, **E:** S
The Love Song, Century Theatre, New York, **P:** Lee Shubert, Jacob J. Shubert, **D:** Fred Latham, **C:** Marguerite Namara, Dorothy Francis, Odette Mirtyl, Evelyn Herbert, 1.13.1925, **E:** S
Im weissen Rössl, Grosses Schauspielhaus, Berlin, **P/D:** Erik Charell, **C:** Camille Spira, Max Hansen, Walter Jankuhn, Otto Wallburg, Trude Lieske, **R:** 11.8.1930, **E:** S
The White Horse Inn, London Coliseum, P/R: Erik Charell, **C:** Clifford Mollison, Lea Seidl, **R:** 4.8.1931, **E:** S. English version of *Im weissen Rössl.*
Nuit de Folies, Folies Bergère, Paris, **P:** Paul Derval, **D:** Louis Lemarchand, **C:** Lemercier, Castel, Mingand, Brochard, **R:** 2.1.1932, **E:** S
L'Auberge du Cheval Blanc, Théâtre Mogador, Paris, **P:** Frères Isola, **D:** Erik Charell, **C:** Rose Carday, Fernand Charpin, Georges Milton, Gabrielle Ristori, **R:** 10.1.1932, **E:** S. French version of *Im weissen Rössl.*

1934–1939: London, Zurich
Here's How!, The Saville Theatre, **P/D:** Austin Melford, **C:** George Robey, Lili Damita, Jack Donohue, **R:** 2.22.1934
Rise and Shine, Theatre Royal, Drury Lane, **P/D:** Ralph Reader, **C:** Binnie Hale, Jack Whiting, Clarice Hardwicke, Irene Browne, **R:** 5.7.1936
Swing Along, The Gaiety Theatre, **P:** Herbert Bryan, Leslie Henson, **D:** Firth Shephard, **C:** Leslie Henson, Louise Browne, Fred Emney, Richard Hearne, **R:** 9.2.1936
Careless Rapture, Theatre Royal, Drury Lane, **P:** Leontine Sagan, **D:** Ralph Reader, **C:** Ivor Novello, Dorothy Dickson, Zena Dare, Olive Gilbert, **R:** 9.11.1936
Balalaika, The Adelphi Theatre, **P/D:** Leontine Sagan, **C:** Muriel Angelus, Clifford Mollison, Roger Treville, Betty Warren, **R:** 12.22.1936
Cinderella, London Coliseum, **P:** Prince Littler, **D:** Stanley Bell, **C:** Edna Best, Madge Elliott, Lupino Lane, Rita Stirling, **R:** 12.24.1936
Darling You, Streatham Hill Theatre, **P:** Prince Littler, **C:** Leslie Fuller, Hal Gordon, Kenneth Kove, **R:** 3.1.1937
New Faces, Metropolitan, **D:** Janice Hart, Frank O'Brian, **C:** Janice Hart, John Lawrence, Frank O'Brian, William Serion, **R:** 6.14.1937
Floodlight, Saville Theatre, **P:** C. Denis Freeman, **C:** Frances Day, John Mills, **R:** 6.23.1937

Crest of the Wave, Theatre Royal, Drury Lane, **P:** Leontine Sagan, **C:** Ivor Novello, Dorothy Dickson, **R:** 9.1.1937
Going Greek, The Gaiety Theatre, **P:** Firth Shephard, **D:** Leslie Henson, **C:** Leslie Henson, Louise Browne, Roy Royston, Fred Emney, Richard Hearne, **R:** 9.16.1937
London Rhapsody, The London Palladium, **P/D:** George Black, **C:** The Crazy Gang, **R:** 9.20.1937
Wild Oats, Prince's Theatre, **P:** Herbert Bryan, Frances Marsden, **C:** Sidney Howard, Arthur Riscoe, Vera Pearce, Josephine Houston, Jack Donohue, **R:** 4.13.1938
Pelissier's Follies of 1938, Saville Theatre, **P:** Anthony Pelissier, Robert Nesbitt, **C:** Rosalie Corneille, Gene Gerrard, Patrick Waddington, **R:** 5.4.1938
Running Riot, The Gaiety Theatre, **P:** Firth Shephard, **D:** Leslie Henson, Herbert Bryan, **C:** Leslie Henson, Louise Browne, Roy Royston, Fred Emney, Richard Hearne, **R:** 8.31.1938
Paprika, His Majesty's Theatre, **P:** Leontine Sagan, **D:** Eric Maschwitz, **C:** Malcolm Keen, Anthony Eustrel, Barbara Bori, Helene Have, **R:** 9.15.1938
Magyar Melody, His Majesty's Theatre, **D:** Eric Maschwitz, Fred Thompson, Guy Bolton, **C:** Lawrence Anderson, Binnie Hale, Barbara Spicer, Anne Allan, Isabel Ohmead, **R:** 1.20.1939
Der verlorene Faden, Modetheater, Schweizerische Landesausstellung 1939, **D:** Max Werner Lenz, **C:** Hortense Raky, Willi Ackermann, Rainer Litten, Max Röthlisberger, **R:** 5.8.1939
Alles Neu, Modetheater, Schweizerische Landesausstellung 1939, **D:** Hans Zimmermann, **C:** Voli Geiler, Hortense Raky, Willi Ackermann, Zarli Carigiet, Karl Meier, Peter W. Staub, **R:** 7.14.1939
Sitting Pretty, Prince's Theatre, **D:** Herbert Bryan, **C:** Jack Donohue, Patricia Burke, Guy Fane, Vera Pearce, Arthur Riscoe, Sidney Howard, **R:** 8.17.1939
Eva, Modetheater, Schweizerische Landesausstellung 1939, **R:** 9.17.1939

1941–1965: Los Angeles, San Francisco, St. Gallen, New York, Zurich, Geneva

Jump for Joy, Mayan Theatre, Los Angeles, **P:** American Revue Theatre, **C:** Duke Ellington and His Orchestra, Ivy Anderson, Dorothy Dandridge, Potts Jackson, Herb Jeffries, Skillet May, Pans Ware, **R:** 7.10.1941
Rosalinda, San Francisco Civic Light Opera, **P:** Edwin Lester, **D:** Eugene Bryden, **C:** Milada Mladova, Irene Manning, Wilbur Evans, Rosemarie Brancato, George Zoritch, **R:** 4.28.1947
The Three Musketeers, Los Angeles Civic Light Opera, **P:** Edwin Lester, **C:** John Tyers, Polyna Stoska, Frances McCann, Marthe Erolle, Carol Haney, **R:** 6.16.1947
Naughty Marietta, Los Angeles Civic Light Opera, **P:** Edwin Lester, **C:** Susanna Foster, Wilbru Evans, Edward Everett Horton, Mitzi Gaynor, **R:** 5.31.1948
Così fan tutte, Stadttheater St. Gallen, **D:** Dr. Kachler, **C:** Heinz Friedrich, Hedda Heusser, Heinz Huggler, Fritz Ollendorf, **R:** 11.1.1955
Swiss Echoes, Radio City Music Hall, New York, **P/D:** Leon Leonidoff, **C:** Geschwister Schmid, **R:** 4.23.1959
The Merry Widow, Los Angeles Civic Light Opera, **P/D:** Edwin Lester, **C:** Patrice Munsel, Bob Wright, Gale Gordon, Jean Fenn, Sig Arno, **R:** 4.17.1961
Die Fledermaus, Stadttheater Zürich, **D:** Herbert Graf, **C:** Rudolf Schock, Adèle Leigh, Ralp Telasko, Regina Sarfaty, Walter Hesse, **R:** 12.31.1961
La Traviata, Grand Théâtre de Genève, **D:** Herbert Graf, **C:** Renata Scotto, Elisabetta Fusco, Luciana Boni, Alfredo Kraus, Licinio Montefusco, **R:** 9.27.1963
The Merry Widow, Lincoln Center, New York, **D:** Richard Rodgers, **C:** Patrice Munsel, Bob Wright, Frank Porretta, Sig Arno, Joan Weldon, **R:** 8.17.1964
La Chauve-Souris, Grand Théâtre de Genève, **D:** Herbert Graf, **C:** Cora Canne Meijer, Teresa Stich-Randall, Oleh De Nyzankovsky, Graziella Sciutti, **R:** 12.28.1965

Films

1924–1928: Hollywood

Monsieur Beaucaire, **D:** Sidney Olcott, **P:** Famous Players-Lasky/Paramount, **C:** Bebe Daniels, Rudolph Valentino, Lois Wilson, **R:** 8.11.1924, **E:** S, U
Madame Sans-Gêne, **D:** Léonce Perret, **P:** Famous Players-Lasky/Paramount, **C:** Émile Drain, Arlette Marchal, Gloria Swanson, **R:** 4.17.1925
The Coast of Folly, **D:** Allan Dwan, **P:** Famous Players-Lasky/Paramount, **C:** Anthony Jowitt, Gloria Swanson, **R:** 8.30.1925
Stage Struck, **D:** Allan Dwan, **P:** Famous Players-Lasky/Paramount, **C:** Lawrence Gray, Gloria Swanson, **R:** 11.16.1925
The Untamed Lady, **D:** Frank Tuttle, **P:** Famous Players-Lasky/Paramount, **C:** Lawrence Gray, Gloria Swanson, **R:** 3.14.1926, **E:** U
Beau Geste, **D:** Herbert Brenton, **P:** Famous Players-Lasky/Paramount, **C:** Ronald Colman, Ralph Forbes, **R:** 8.25.1926, **E:** U
The Love of Sunya, **D:** Albert Parker, **P:** Famous Players-Lasky/Paramount, **C:** John Boles, Gloria Swanson, **R:** 3.11.1927
Mr. Wu, **D:** William Nigh, **P:** Metro-Goldwyn-Mayer, **C:** Renée Adorée, Lon Chaney, Louise Dresser, **R:** 3.26.1927, **E:** U
Frisco Sally Levy, **D:** William Beaudine, **P:** Metro-Goldwyn-Mayer, **C:** Roy D'Arcv, Sally O'Neil, **R:** 4.2.1927
The Callahans and the Murphys, **D:** George W. Hill, **P:** Metro-Goldwyn-Mayer, **C:** Marie Dressler, Poly Moran, Sally O'Neil, **R:** 5.11.1927
On Ze Boulevard, **D:** Harry F. Millarde, **P:** Metro-Goldwyn-Mayer, **C:** Lew Cody, Renée Adorée, **R:** 5.25.1927
Twelve Miles Out, **D:** Jack Conway, **P:** Metro-Goldwyn-Mayer, **C:** Joan Crawford, John Gilbert, Ernest Torrence, **R:** 6.9.1927
Adam and Evil, **D:** Robert Z. Leonard, **P:** Metro-Goldwyn-Mayer, **C:** Lew Cody, Aileen Pringle, **R:** 8.8.1927
After Midnight, **D:** Monta Bell, **P:** Metro-Goldwyn-Mayer, **C:** Lawrence Gray, Norma Shearer, **R:** 8.15.1927
Foreign Devils, **D:** W.S. Van Dyke, **P:** Metro-Goldwyn-Mayer, **C:** Tim McCoy, Claire Windsor, **R:** 9.3.1927
Body and Soul, **D:** Reginald Barker, **P:** Metro-Goldwyn-Mayer, **C:** Lionel Barrymore, Norman Kerry, Aileen Pringle, **R:** 10.1.1927
Quality Street, **D:** Sidney Franklin, **P:** Metro-Goldwyn-Mayer, **C:** Marion Davies, Conrad Nagel, **R:** 11.1.1927
Love, **D:** Edmund Goulding, **P:** Metro-Goldwyn-Mayer, **C:** Greta Garbo, John Gilbert, **R:** 11.29.1927, **E:** S, U
Sadie Thompson, **D:** Raoul Walsh, **P:** Gloria Swanson Pictures, **C:** Lionel Barrymore, Gloria Swanson, **R:** 1.7.1928, **E:** A
The Wind, **D:** Victor Sjöström, **P:** Metro-Goldwyn-Mayer, **C:** Lilian Gish, Lars Hanson, **R:** 9.17.1928, **E:** U

1928–1930: Berlin, Paris

La danseuse Orchidée, **D:** Léonce Perret, **P:** Franco Films, **C:** Ricardo Cortez, Xenia Desni, Louise Lagrange, **R:** 4.29.1928, **E:** U

Ungarische Rhapsodie, **D:** Hanns Schwarz, **P:** Universum Film, **C:** Lil Dagover, Dita Parlo, Willy Fritsch, **R:** 11.5.1928, **E:** A

Asphalt, **D:** Joe May, **P:** Universum Film, **C:** Betty Amann, Gustav Fröhlich, **R:** 3.12.1929

Die wunderbare Lüge der Nina Petrowna, **D:** Hanns Schwarz, **P:** Universum Film, **C:** Brigitte Helm, Francis Lederer, Warwick Ward, **R:** 4.15.1929

Manolescu – Der König der Hochstapler, **D:** Viktor Tourjansky, **P:** Universum Film, **C:** Heinrich George, Brigitte Helm, Ivan Mozzhukhin, **R:** 8.22.1929

The Trespasser, **D:** Edmund Goulding, **P:** Gloria Productions/United Artists, **C:** Robert Ames, Gloria Swanson, **R:** 11.11.1929, **E:** S, U. Hubert sent his designs from Berlin to Hollywood, where Swanson had them revised by her seamstress Ann Morgan.

Liebeswalzer, **D:** Wilhelm Thiele, **P:** Universum Film, **C:** Willy Fritsch, Lilian Harvey, **R:** 2.7.1930

Valse d'amour, **D:** Wilhelm Thiele, **P:** Universum Film, **C:** Willy Fritsch, Lilian Harvey, **R:** 2.7.1930, **E:** U, French version of *Liebeswalzer*

Sous les toits de Paris, **D:** René Clair, **P:** Films Sonores Tobis, **C:** Pola Illéry, Gaston Modot, Albert Préjean, **R:** 4.28.1930

Hokuspokus, **D:** Gustav Ucicky, **P:** Universum Film, **C:** Willy Fritsch, Lilian Harvey, **R:** 7.11.1930, **E:** Hubert as an actor in a supporting role

The Love Waltz, **D:** Wilhelm Thiele, **P:** Universum Film, **C:** John Batten, Lilian Harvey, **R:** 7.23.1930, **E:** English version of *Liebeswalzer*

Die Drei von der Tankstelle, **D:** Wilhelm Thiele, **P:** Universum Film, **C:** Willy Fritsch, Lilian Harvey, Oskar Karlweis, Heinz Rühmann, **R:** 9.15.1930

Liebling der Götter, **D:** Hanns Schwarz, **P:** Universum Film, **C:** Emil Jannings, Renate Müller, **R:** 10.13.1930

The Temporary Widow, **D:** Gustav Ucicky, **P:** Universum Film, **C:** Lilian Harvey, Laurence Olivier, **R:** 10.20.1930, **E:** Hubert in a supporting role, English version of *Hokuspokus*

Le chemin du paradis, **D:** Wilhelm Thiele/Max de Vaucorbeil, **P:** Universum Film, **C:** Henri Garat, Lilian Harvey, René Levèvre, Jacques Maury, **R:** 11.14.1930, **E:** U, French version of *Die Drei von der Tankstelle*

1930–1931: Hollywood

What a Widow!, **D:** Allan Dwan, **P:** Gloria Productions/United Artists, **C:** Lew Cody, Owen Moore, Gloria Swanson, **R:** 9.13.1930

Those Three French Girls, **D:** Harry Beaumont, **P:** Metro-Goldwyn-Mayer, **C:** Fifi D'Orsay, Yola d'Avril, Sandra Ravel, **R:** 10.11.1930

War Nurse, **D:** Edgar Selwyn, **P:** Metro-Goldwyn-Mayer, **C:** Robert Ames, Robert Montgomery, June Walker, **R:** 10.22.1930

Min and Bill, **D:** George W. Hill, **P:** Metro-Goldwyn-Mayer, **C:** Marie Dressler, Wallace Beery, **R:** 11.21.1930

Reducing, **D:** Charles Reisner, **P:** Metro-Goldwyn-Mayer, **C:** Marie Dressler, Polly Morgan, **R:** 1.3.1931

The Great Meadow, **D:** Charles Brabin, **P:** Metro-Goldwyn-Mayer, **C:** Eleanor Boardman, Gavin Gordon, Johnny Mack Brown, **R:** 1.24.1931

Mordprozess Mary Dugan, **P:** Metro-Goldwyn-Mayer, **C:** Hermann Bing, Nora Gregor, **R:** 2.3.1931, **E:** U, German version of *The Trial of Mary Dugan*

The Easiest Way, **D:** Jack Conway, **P:** Metro-Goldwyn-Mayer, **C:** Constance Bennett, Adolphe Menjou, Robert Montgomery, **R:** 2.7.1931

The Prodigal, **D:** Harry A. Pollard, **P:** Metro-Goldwyn-Mayer, **C:** Lawrence Tibbett, Esther Ralston, **R:** 2.21.1931

Parlor, Bedroom and Bath, **D:** Edward Sedgwick, **P:** Metro-Goldwyn-Mayer, **C:** Reginald Denny, Charlotte Greenwood, Buster Keaton, **R:** 2.28.1931

Gentleman's Fate, **D:** Mervyn LeRoy, **P:** Metro-Goldwyn-Mayer, **C:** John Gilbert, Leila Hyams, Louis Wolheim, **R:** 3.7.1931

La fruta amarga, 1931, **D:** Arthur Gregor/José López Rubio, **P:** Metro-Goldwyn-Mayer, **C:** Virginia Fábgregas, Juan de Landa, **R:** 3.13.1931, **E:** A, Spanish Version of *Min and Bill*

Men Call It Love, **D:** Edgar Selwyn, **P:** Metro-Goldwyn-Mayer, **C:** Leila Hyams, Adolphe Menjou, **R:** 3.14.1931

A Tailor Made Man, **D:** Sam Wood, **P:** Metro-Goldwyn-Mayer, **C:** William Haines, **R:** 3.28.1931, **E:** U

Stepping Out, **D:** Charles Reisner, **P:** Metro-Goldwyn-Mayer, **C:** Reginald Denny, Charlotte Greenwood, Leila Hyams, **R:** 4.11.1931

The Secret 6, **D:** George W. Hill, **P:** Metro-Goldwyn-Mayer, **C:** Wallace Beery, Jean Harlow, Johnny Mack Brown, Lewis Stone, **R:** 4.18.1931

Indiscreet, **D:** Leo McCarey, **P:** Feature Productions/United Artists, **C:** Gloria Swanson, Ben Lyon, Monroe Owsley, **R:** 25.4.1931

Shipmates, **D:** Harry A. Pollard, **P:** Metro-Goldwyn-Mayer, **C:** Dorothy Jordan, Robert Montgomery, Ernest Torrence, **R:** 25.4.1931

Daybreak, **D:** Jacques Feyder, **P:** Metro-Goldwyn-Mayer, **C:** Helen Chandler, Jean Hersholt, Ramon Novarro, **R:** 5.2.1931

Never the Twain Shall Meet, **D:** W. S. Van Dyke, **P:** Metro-Goldwyn-Mayer, **C:** Conchita Montenegro, Leslie Howard, **R:** 5.16.1931

The Great Lover, **D:** Harry Beaumont, **P:** Metro-Goldwyn-Mayer, **C:** Adolphe Menjou, Irene Dunne, **R:** 5.18.1931

Cheri-Bibi, **D:** Carlos F. Borcosque, Metro-Goldwyn-Mayer, **C:** Ernesto Vilches, María Fernanda Ladrón de Guevara, María Tubau, **R:** 5.30.1931, **E:** A

Just a Gigolo, **D:** Jack Conway, **P:** Metro-Goldwyn-Mayer, **C:** William Haines, Irene Purcell, **R:** 6.6.1931

El proceso de Mary Dugan, **D:** Marcel De Sano, **P:** Metro-Goldwyn-Mayer, **C:** José Crespo, María Fernanda Ladrón de Guevara, **R:** 6.26.1931, **E:** A, Spanish version of *The Trial of Mary Dugan*

Son of India, **D:** Jacques Feyder, **P:** Metro-Goldwyn-Mayer, **C:** Madge Evans, Ramón Novarro, **R:** 8.1.1931

Le fils du rajah, **D:** Claude Autant-Lara, **P:** Metro-Goldwyn-Mayer, **R:** 8.1.1931, **E:** A, French version of *Son of India*

Guilty Hands, **D:** W.S. Van Dyke, **P:** Metro-Goldwyn-Mayer, **C:** Lionel Barrymore, Madge Evans, Kay Francis, **R:** 8.22.1931

The Phantom of Paris, **D:** John S. Robertson, **P:** Metro-Goldwyn-Mayer, **C:** John Gilbert, Leila Hyams, **R:** 9.12.1931, **E:** English Version of *Cheri-Bibi*

The Sin of Madelon Claudet, **D:** Edgar Selwyn, **P:** Metro-Goldwyn-Mayer, **C:** Helen Hayes, Lewis Stone, **R:** 10.23.1931

Le procès de Mary Dugan, **D:** Marcel De Sano, **P:** Metro-Goldwyn-Mayer, **C:** Charles Boyer, Huguette Duflos, **R:** 11.6.1931, **E:** U, French version of *The Trial of Mary Dugan*

Buster se marie, **D:** Claude Autant-Lara, **P:** Metro-Goldwyn-Mayer, **C:** Jeanne Helbling, Buster Keaton, André Luguet, Françoise Rosay, **R:** 12.23.1931, **E:** U, A, French version of *Parlor, Bedroom and Bath*
Shanghai Express, **D:** Josef von Sternberg, **P:** Paramount, **C:** Clive Brook, Marlene Dietrich, **R:** 2.4.1932, **E:** S, U
Casanova wider Willen, **D:** Edward Brophy, **P:** Metro-Goldwyn-Mayer, **C:** Buster Keaton, Marion Lessing, Paul Morgan, Françoise Rosay, **R:** 2.15.1932, **E:** A, German version of *Parlor, Bedroom and Bath*
Quand on est belle, **D:** Arthur Robison, **P:** Metro-Goldwyn-Mayer, **C:** Lili Damita, André Luguet, Françoise Rosay, **R:** 3.25.1932, **E:** A, French version of *The Easiest Way*
Flesh, **D:** John Ford, **P:** Metro-Goldwyn-Mayer, **C:** Wallace Beery, Ricardo Cortez, Karen Morley, **R:** 12.3.1932, **E:** U

1931–1934: Paris, Berlin

Bomben auf Monte Carlo, **D:** Hanns Schwarz, **P:** Universum Film, **C:** Hans Albers, Heinz Rühmann, Anna Sten, **R:** 8.31.1931
Le capitaine Craddock, **D:** Hanns Schwarz, **P:** Universum Film, **C:** Jean Murat, Käthe von Nagy, **R:** 12.4.1931, **E:** French version of *Bomben auf Monte Carlo*
À nous la liberté, **D:** René Clair, **P:** Films Sonores Tobis, **C:** Raymond Cordy, Rolla France, Henri Marchand, **R:** 12.18.1931
La chance, **D:** René Guissart, **P:** Les Studios Paramount, **C:** Marie Bell, Marcel André, **R:** 12.24.1931, **E:** U
Stürme der Leidenschaft, **D:** Robert Siodmak, **P:** Universum Film, **C:** Emil Jannings, Anna Sten, **R:** 1.22.1932
Die nackte Wahrheit, **D:** Karl Anton, **P:** Les Studios Paramount, **C:** Jenny Jugo, Oskar Karlweis, Otto Wernicke **R:** 1.31.1932, **E:** A
Tu seras Duchesse, **D:** René Guissart, **P:** Les Studios Paramount, **C:** Marie Glory, Fernand Gravey, **R:** 2.12.1932, **E:** U
Il est charmant, **D:** Louis Mercanton, **P:** Les Studios Paramount, **C:** Henri Garat, Meg Lemonnier, **R:** 2.25.1932, **E:** U
Monte Carlo Madness, **D:** Hanns Schwarz, **P:** Universum Film, **C:** Hans Albers, Helen Haye, Sari Maritza, **R:** 3.23.1932, **E:** A, English version of *Bomben auf Monte Carlo*
Studenter i Paris, **D:** Louis Mercanton, **P:** Les Studios Paramount, **C:** Henri Garat, Meg Lemonnier, **R:** 4.13.1932, **E:** A, Swedish version of *Il est charmant*
Tumultes, **D:** Robert Siodmak, **P:** Universum Film, **C:** Charles Boyer, Florelle, Armand Bernard, **R:** 4.22.1932, **E:** French version of *Stürme der Leidenschaft*
Miche, **D:** Jean de Marguenat, **P:** Les Studios Paramount, **C:** Robert Burnier, Edith Méra, Marguerite Moreno, Suzy Vernon, **R:** 4.28.1932, **E:** U
Une nuit à l'hôtel, **D:** Leo Mittler, **P:** Les Studios Paramount, **C:** Marcelle Romée, Willy Rozier, Betty Stockfeld, **R:** 5.15.1932, **E:** U
Avec l'assurance, **D:** Roger Capellani, **P:** Les Studios Paramount, **C:** Jeanne Helbling, Madeleine Guitty, Saint-Granier, **R:** 5.16.1932, **E:** U
Coiffeur pour dames, R : René Guissart, **P:** Les Studios Paramount, **C:** Mona Goya, Nina Myral, Laure Diana, Simone Héliard, **R:** 5.20.1932, **E:** A
Monsieur Albert, **D:** Karl Anton, **P:** Les Studios Paramount, **C:** Edwige Feuillère, Noël-Noël, Betty Stockfeld, **R:** 6.2.1932, **E:** S, U
Cognasse, **D:** Louis Mercanton, **P:** Les Studios Paramount, **C:** Thérèse Dorny, Marguerite Moreno, Tramel, **R:** 9.1.1932, **E:** A
Passionnément, **D:** René Guissart, **P:** Les Studios Paramount, **C:** Florelle, Fernand Gravey, **R:** 9.20.1932, **E:** U
Mon cœur balance, **D:** René Guissart, **P:** Les Studios Paramount, **C:** Marie Glory, Marguerite Moreno, Noël-Noël, Hélène Perdrière, **R:** 10.27.1932, **E:** A
Le fils improvisé, **D:** René Guissart, **P:** Les Studios Paramount, **C:** Florelle, Fernand Gravey, **R:** 11.22.1932, **E:** U
La belle marinière, **D:** Harry Lachman, **P:** Les Studios Paramount, **C:** Rosine Deréan, Jean Gabin, Madeleine Renaud **R:** 12.2.1932, **E:** A
Pour vivre heureux, **D:** Claudio de la Torre, **P:** Les Studios Paramount, **C:** Noël-Noël, Suzet Maïs, Simone Simon, **R:** 12.16.1932, **E:** A
Perfect Understanding, **D:** Cyril Gardner, **P:** Gloria Swanson British Productions, **C:** John Halliday, Laurence Olivier, Gloria Swanson, **R:** 1.1.1933, **E:** S, U
Topaze, **D:** Louis J. Gasnier, **P:** Les Studios Paramount, **C:** Edwige Feuillère, Louis Jouvet, Paul Pauley, **R:** 1.6.1933, **E:** S, U
Quatorze Juillet, **D:** René Clair, **P:** Films Sonores Tobis, **C:** Annabella, George Rigaud, **R:** 1.14.1933
La pouponnière, **D:** Jean Boyer, **P:** Les Studios Paramount, **C:** Robert Arnoux, Germaine Roger, Françoise Rosay, **R:** 2.3.1933, **E:** U
Le Chausseur de chez Maxim's, **D:** Karl Anton, **P:** Les Studios Paramount, **C:** Tramel, Suzy Vernon, **R:** 3.2.1933, **E:** U
Une faible femme, **D:** Max de Vaucorbeil, **P:** Les Studios Paramount, **C:** Meg Lemonnier, André Luguet, **R:** 3.17.1933, **E:** U
Rien que des mensonges, **D:** Karl Anton, **P:** Les Studios Paramount, **C:** Raymonde Allain, Janine Guise, Jackie Monnier, Marguerite Moreno, **R:** 5.16.1933, **E:** A
Walzerkrieg, **D:** Ludwig Berger, **P:** Universum Film, **C:** Willy Fritsch, Renate Müller, **R:** 10.4.1933
La guerre des valses, **D:** Ludwig Berger, **P:** Universum Film, **C:** Dranem, Fernand Gravey, Madeleine Ozeray, **R:** 12.12.1933, A: French version of *Walzerkrieg*
Simone est comme ça, **D:** Max de Vaucorbeil, **P:** Les Studios Paramount, **C:** Henri Garat, Meg Lemonnier, **R:** 12.29.1933, **E:** U
Volga en flammes, **D:** Viktor Tourjansky, **P:** AB/Films Charles Philipp/Omnia Paris, Februar 1934, **C:** Danielle Darrieux, Albert Préjean, Raymond Rouleau, **R:** 2.9.1934
On a volé un homme, **D:** Max Ophüls, **P:** Les Productions Fox Europa, **C:** Lili Damita, Charles Fallot, **R:** 3.13.1934, **E:** U
Sapho, **D:** Léonce Perret, **P:** Pathé-Natan, **C:** Mary Marquet, Jean-Max, **R:** 4.7.1934, **E:** U
Liliom, **D:** Fritz Lang, **P:** Les Productions Fox Europa, **C:** Charles Boyer, Florelle, Madeleine Ozeray, **R:** 4.27.1934

1934–1935: Hollywood

Servants' Entrance, **D:** Frank Lloyd, **P:** Fox Film, **C:** Lew Ayres, Janet Gaynor, **R:** 9.26.1934
Marie Galante, **D:** Henry King, **P:** Fox Film, **C:** Ketti Gallian, Spencer Tracy, **R:** 10.26.1934
Elinor Norton, **D:** Hamilton MacFadden, **P:** Fox Film, **C:** Norman Foster, Claire Trevor, Hugh Williams, **R:** 11.2.1934
Hell in the Heavens, **D:** John G. Blystone, Fox Film, **C:** Warner Baxter, Russell Hardie, Conchita Montenegro, **R:** 12.12.1934, **E:** S, U
Music in the Air, **D:** Joe May, **P:** Fox Film, **C:** John Boles, Douglass Montgomery, Gloria Swanson, **R:** 12.13.1934
The Lottery Lover, **D:** Wilhelm Thiele, **P:** Fox Film, **C:** Lew Ayres, Peggy Fears, Pat Paterson, **R:** 2.5.1935
One More Spring, **D:** Henry King, **P:** Fox Film, **C:** Warner Baxter, Janet Gaynor, **R:** 2.12.1935, **E:** S, U

It's a Small World, **D:** Henry King, **P:** Fox Film, **C:** Wendy Barrie, Spencer Tracy, Raymond Walburn, **R:** 4.12.1935
Our Little Girl, **D:** John S. Robertson, **P:** Fox Film, **C:** Rosemary Ames, Joel McCrea, Shirley Temple, **R:** 5.17.1935
Under the Pampas Moon, **D:** James Tinling, **P:** Fox Film, **C:** Warner Baxter, Ketti Gallian, **R:** 6.1.1935
Spring Tonic, **D:** Clyde Bruckman, **P:** Fox Film, **C:** Lew Ayres, Claire Trevor, **R:** 6.27.1935
Doubting Thomas, **D:** David Butler, **P:** Fox Film, **C:** Billie Burke, Will Rogers, **R:** 7.10.1935
The Daring Young Man, **D:** William A. Seiter, **P:** Fox Film, **C:** Mae Clarke, James Dunn, Neil Hamilton, **R:** 7.18.1935
Curly Top, **D:** Irving Cummings, **P:** Fox Film, **C:** John Boles, Rochelle Hudson, Shirley Temple, **R:** 7.26.1935
The Farmer Takes a Wife, **D:** Victor Fleming, **P:** Fox Film, **C:** Henry Fonda, Janet Gaynor, **R:** 8.2.1935
Orchids to You, **D:** William A. Seiter, **P:** Fox Film, **C:** John Boles, Jean Muir, **R:** 8.10.1935
Here's to Romance, **D:** Alfred E. Green, **P:** Jesse L. Lasky Productions/Fox Film, **C:** Anita Louise, Nino Martini, Genevieve Tobin, **R:** 8.27.1935
Redheads on Parade, **D:** Norman Z. McLeod, **P:** Fox Film, **C:** John Boles, Dixie Lee, **R:** 8.30.1935, **E:** S, U
Dressed to Thrill, **D:** Harry Lachman, **P:** Fox Film, **C:** Robert Barrat, Clive Brook, Tutta Rolf, **R:** 10.8.1935, **E:** S, U

1935–1939: London

The Ghost Goes West, **D:** René Clair, **P:** London Films, **C:** Robert Donat, Eugene Pallette, Jean Parker, **R:** 12.17.1935
Things to Come, **D:** William Cameron Menzies, **P:** London Films, **C:** Pearl Argyle, Raymond Massey, Ralph Richardson, Margaretta Scott, **R:** 2.21.1936
Dishonour Bright, **D:** Tom Walls, **P:** Cecil Films/Capitol Film, **C:** Diana Churchill, Betty Stockfeld, Tom Walls, **R:** 9.22.1936, **E:** U
Rembrandt, **D:** Alexander Korda, **P:** London Films, **C:** Elsa Lancaster, Charles Laughton, Gertrude Lawrence, **R:** 11.9.1936, **E:** S, U
Men Are Not Gods, **D:** Walter Reisch, **P:** London Films, **C:** Miriam Hopkins, Gertrude Lawrence, Sebastian Shaw, **R:** 11.26.1936
Fire over England, **D:** William K. Howard, **P:** London Films, **C:** Vivien Leigh, Laurence Olivier, Flora Robson, **R:** 1.8.1937
Dark Journey, **D:** Victor Saville, **P:** London Films, **C:** Vivien Leigh, Conrad Veidt, **R:** 1.30.1937
Wings of the Morning, **D:** Harold D. Schuster, **P:** New World Pictures, **C:** Annabella, Leslie Banks, Henry Fonda, **R:** 2.1.1937, **E:** U
Elephant Boy, **D:** Alexander Korda, **P:** London Films, **C:** Sabu, W. E. Holloway, Walter Hudd, **R:** 2.8.1937, **E:** A
Farewell Again, **D:** Tim Whelan, **P:** London Films, **C:** Leslie Banks, Flora Robson, **R:** 5.15.1937
Under the Red Robe, **D:** Victor Sjöström, **P:** New World Pictures, **C:** Annabella, Raymond Massey, Conrad Veidt, **R:** 5.25.1937
Knight without Armour, **D:** Jacques Feyder, **P:** London Films, **C:** Marlene Dietrich, Robert Donat, **R:** 6.1.1937, **E:** S, U
The Return of the Scarlet Pimpernel, **D:** Hanns Schwarz, **P:** London Films, **C:** Barry K. Barnes, James Mason, Sophie Stewart, Margaretta Scott, **R:** 10.20.1937
Dinner at the Ritz, **D:** Harold D. Schuster, **P:** New World Pictures, **C:** Annabella, Romney Brent, Paul Lukas, David Niven, **R:** 10.21.1937
Paradise for Two, **D:** Harold D. Schuster, **P:** London Films, **C:** Patricia Ellis, Jack Hulbert, **R:** 12.22.1937, **E:** US title: *The Gaiety Girls*
The Divorce of Lady X, **D:** Tim Whelan, **P:** London Films, **C:** Merle Oberon, Laurence Olivier, **R:** 1.13.1938
Sweet Devil, **D:** Tim Whelan, **P:** Jack Buchanan/General Film, **C:** Jean Gillie, Bobby Howes, William Kendall, **R:** 2.1.1938
A Yank at Oxford, **D:** Jack Conway, **P:** Metro-Goldwyn-Mayer, **C:** Lionel Barrymore, Vivien Leigh, Maureen O'Sullivan, Robert Taylor, **R:** 2.18.1938
The Drum, **D:** Zoltan Korda, **P:** London Films, **C:** Sabu, Raymond Massey, **R:** 4.7.1938
Break the News, **D:** René Clair, **P:** London Films, **C:** Jack Buchanan, Maurice Chevalier, June Knight, **R:** 5.19.1938
The Sky's the Limit, **D:** Jack Buchanan, **P:** London Films, **C:** Jack Buchanan, William Kendall, Mara Losseff, **R:** 6.1.1938
Over the Moon, **D:** Thornton Freeland, **P:** London Films, **C:** Rex Harrison, Merle Oberon, **R:** 2.12.1939
So This Is London, **D:** Thornton Freeland, **P:** 20th Century-Fox, **C:** Fay Compton, Alfred Drayton, Robertson Hare, George Sanders, **R:** 3.30.1939, **E:** U
The Four Feathers, **D:** Zoltan Korda, **P:** London Films, **C:** John Clements, June Duprez, Ralph Richardson, C. Aubrey Smith, **R:** 4.17.1939

1941–1950: Hollywood

That Hamilton Woman, **D:** Alexander Korda, **P:** Alexander Korda Films, **C:** Vivien Leigh, Laurence Olivier, **R:** 4.3.1941
The Flame of New Orleans, **D:** René Clair, **P:** Universal, **C:** Bruce Cabot, Marlene Dietrich, Roland Young, **R:** 4.24.1941
New Wine, **D:** Reinhold Schünzel, **P:** Gloria Pictures, **C:** Alan Curtis, Ilona Massey, **R:** 9.10.1941
Lydia, **D:** Julien Duvivier, **P:** Alexander Korda Films, **C:** Merle Oberon, Joseph Cotten, Edna May Oliver, **R:** 9.18.1941, **E:** U
Father Takes a Wife, **D:** Jack Hively, **P:** RKO Radio Pictures, **C:** Adolphe Menjou, Gloria Swanson, **R:** 11.4.1941
Twin Beds, **D:** Tim Whelan, **P:** Edward Small Productions, **C:** Joan Bennett, George Brent, **R:** 4.30.1942
The Pride of the Yankees, **D:** Sam Wood, **P:** Samuel Goldwyn/RKO Radio Pictures, **C:** Walter Brennan, Gary Cooper, Babe Ruth, Teresa Wright, **R:** 7.15.1942
The Powers Girl, **D:** Norman Z. McLeod, **P:** Charles R. Rogers Productions, **C:** Carole Landis, George Murphy, Anne Shirley, **R:** 1.15.1943
Bomber's Moon, **D:** Edward Ludwig (Charles Fuhr), **P:** 20th Century-Fox, **C:** Annabella, George Montgomery, **R:** 7.19.1943
Heaven Can Wait, **D:** Ernst Lubitsch, **P:** 20th Century-Fox, **C:** Don Ameche, Charles Coburn, Gene Tierney, **R:** 8.5.1943
Holy Matrimony, **D:** John M. Stahl, **P:** 20th Century-Fox, **C:** Gracie Fields, Monty Woolley, **R:** 8.27.1943
Wintertime, **D:** John Brahm, **P:** 20th Century-Fox, **C:** Sonja Henie, Jack Oakie, Cesar Romero, **R:** 9.17.1943
Sweet Rosie O'Grady, **D:** Irving Cummings, **P:** 20th Century-Fox, **C:** Betty Grable, Adolphe Menjou, Robert Young, **R:** 10.1.1943
Paris After Dark, **D:** Léonide Moguy, **P:** 20th Century-Fox, **C:** Philip Dorn, Brenda Marshall, George Sanders, **R:** 10.6.1943
Claudia, **D:** Edmund Goulding, **P:** 20th Century-Fox, **C:** Ina Claire, Dorothy McGuire, Robert Young, **R:** 11.4.1943
Happy Land, **D:** Irving Pichel, **P:** 20th Century-Fox, **C:** Don Ameche, Harry Carey, Frances Dee, Ann Rutherford, **R:** 11.10.1943

The Song of Bernadette, **D:** Henry King, **P:** 20th Century-Fox, **C:** Jennifer Jones, **R:** 12.21.1943
Jane Eyre, **D:** Robert Stevenson, **P:** 20th Century-Fox, **C:** Joan Fontaine, Orson Welles, **R:** 12.24.1943
Lifeboat, **D:** Alfred Hitchcock, **P:** 20th Century-Fox, **C:** Mary Anderson, Tallulah Bankhead, William Bendix, John Hodiak, Walter Slezak, **R:** 1.11.1944
The Lodger, **D:** John Brahm, **P:** 20th Century-Fox, **C:** Laird Cregar, Merle Oberon, George Sanders, **R:** 1.19.1944
The Sullivans, **D:** Lloyd Bacon, **P:** 20th Century-Fox, **C:** Anne Baxter, Thomas Mitchell, **R:** 2.3.1944
It Happened Tomorrow, **D:** René Clair, **P:** Arnold Pressburger Films, **C:** Linda Darnell, Jack Oakie, Dick Powell, **R:** 3.27.1944
Buffalo Bill, **D:** William A. Wellman, **P:** 20th Century-Fox, **C:** Linda Darnell, Joel McCrea, Maureen O'Hara, **R:** 4.13.1944
Pin Up Girl, **D:** H. Bruce Humberstone, **P:** 20th Century-Fox, **C:** Betty Grable, John Harvey, Martha Raye, **R:** 4.25.1944
Wilson, **D:** Henry King, **P:** 20th Century-Fox, **C:** Mary Anderson, Charles Coburn, Geraldine Fitzgerald, Ruth Nelson, **R:** 8.1.1944
Laura, **D:** Otto Preminger, **P:** 20th Century-Fox, **C:** Dana Andrews, Gene Tierney, **R:** 10.11.1944, **E:** When Rouben Mamoulian had to hand over the direction to Preminger, Hubert's costumes were also replaced.
Irish Eyes Are Smiling, **D:** Henry King, **P:** 20th Century-Fox, **C:** June Haver, Dick Haymes, Monty Woolley, **R:** 10.19.1944
Dark Waters, **D:** André De Toth, **P:** 20th Century-Fox, **C:** Thomas Mitchell, Merle Oberon, Franchot Tone, **R:** 11.21.1944
Hangover Square, **D:** John Brahm, **P:** 20th Century-Fox, **C:** Laird Cregar, Linda Darnell, George Sanders, **R:** 2.7.1945
A Royal Scandal, **D:** Otto Preminger, **P:** 20th Century-Fox, **C:** Tallulah Bankhead, Anne Baxter, Charles Coburn, William Eythe, **R:** 2.26.1945
Diamond Horseshoe, **D:** George Seaton, **P:** 20th Century-Fox, **C:** Betty Grable, Dick Haymes, **R:** 5.2.1945
Nob Hill, **D:** Henry Hathaway, **P:** 20th Century-Fox, **C:** Joan Bennett, Vivian Blaine, Peggy Ann Garner, George Raft, **R:** 6.13.1945
Captain Eddie, **D:** Lloyd Bacon, **P:** 20th Century-Fox, **C:** Lynn Bari, Fred MacMurray, **R:** 6.19.1945
State Fair, **D:** Lloyd Bacon, **P:** 20th Century-Fox, **C:** Dana Andrews, Jeanne Crain, Vivian Blaine, Dick Haymes, **R:** 8.29.1945
And Then There Were None, **D:** René Clair, **P:** 20th Century-Fox, **C:** June Duprez, Barry Fitzgerald, Louis Hayward, Walter Huston, **R:** 10.31.1945, **E:** U
The Spider, **D:** Robert D. Webb, **P:** 20th Century-Fox, **C:** Richard Conte, Faye Marlowe, Kurt Kreuger, **R:** 12.1.1945
Dragonwyck, **D:** Joseph L. Mankiewicz, 20th Century-Fox, **C:** Walter Huston, Glenn Langan, Vincent Price, Gene Tierney, **R:** 4.10.1946
Do You Love Me, **D:** Gregory Ratoff, **P:** 20th Century-Fox, **C:** Dock Haymes, Harry James, Maureen O'Hara, **R:** 5.17.1946, **E:** S, U
Centennial Summer, **D:** Otto Preminger, **P:** 20th Century-Fox, **C:** Jeanne Crain, Linda Darnell, Cornel Wilde, **R:** 7.10.1946
My Darling Clementine, **D:** John Ford, **P:** 20th Century-Fox, **C:** Linda Darnell, Henry Fonda, Victor Mature, **R:** 10.19.1946
Wake Up and Dream, **D:** Lloyd Bacon, **P:** 20th Century-Fox, **C:** June Haver, John Payne, **R:** 12.2.1946
13 Rue Madeleine, **D:** Henry Hathaway, **P:** 20th Century-Fox, **C:** Annabella, James Cagney, **R:** 1.15.1947
The Late George Apley, **D:** Joseph L. Mankiewicz, **P:** 20th Century-Fox, **C:** Edna Best, Ronald Colman, Peggy Cummins, **R:** 3.20.1947
Carnival in Costa Rica, **D:** Gregory Ratoff, **P:** 20th Century-Fox, **C:** Dick Haymes, Celeste Holm, Cesar Romero, Vera-Ellen, **R:** 3.28.1947
Moss Rose, **D:** Gregory Ratoff, **P:** 20th Century-Fox, **C:** Ethel Barrymore, Peggy Cummins, Victor Mature, **R:** 5.30.1947
The Foxes of Harrow, **D:** John M. Stahl, **P:** 20th Century-Fox, **C:** Rex Harrison, Maureen O'Hara, Vanessa Brown, **R:** 9.24.1947
Forever Amber, **D:** Otto Preminger, **P:** 20th Century-Fox, **C:** Linda Darnell, Cornel Wilde, George Sanders, **R:** 10.22.1947
Fury at Furnace Creek, **D:** H. Bruce Humberstone, **P:** 20th Century-Fox, **C:** Victor Mature, Coleen Gray, **R:** 4.30.1948
Green Grass of Wyoming, **D:** Louis King, **P:** 20th Century-Fox, **C:** Robert Arthur, Charles Coburn, Peggy Cummins, Marilyn Monroe, **R:** 6.3.1948
That Lady in Ermine, **D:** Ernst Lubitsch, **P:** 20th Century-Fox, **C:** Betty Grable, Douglas Fairbanks Jr., Cesar Romero, **R:** 8.24.1948
When My Baby Smiles at Me, **D:** Walter Lang, **P:** 20th Century-Fox, **C:** Dan Dailey, Betty Grable, June Havoc, **R:** 11.10.1948
The Fan, **D:** Otto Preminger, **P:** 20th Century-Fox, **C:** Jeanne Crain, Madeleine Carroll, Richard Greene, George Sanders, **R:** 4.1.1949
The Beautiful Blonde from Bashful Bend, **D:** Preston Sturges, **P:** 20th Century-Fox, **C:** Betty Grable, Cesar Romero, Rudy Vallee, **R:** 5.27.1949
Oh, You Beautiful Doll, **D:** John M. Stahl, **P:** 20th Century-Fox, **C:** June Haver, Mark Stevens, **R:** 11.11.1949
Prince of Foxes, **D:** Henry King, **P:** 20th Century-Fox, **C:** Tyrone Power, Orson Welles, Wanda Hendrix, **R:** 12.23.1949, **E:** The film was made in Italy, where Hubert's Hollywood designs were replaced by those of Vittorio Nino Novarese.
A Ticket to Tomahawk, **D:** Richard Sale, **P:** 20th Century-Fox, **C:** Anne Baxter, Dan Dailey, Marilyn Monroe, **R:** 4.18.1950
Love That Brute, **D:** Alexander Hall, **P:** 20th Century-Fox, **C:** Paul Douglas, Jean Peters, **R:** 5.26.1950
Broken Arrow, **D:** Delmer Daves, **P:** 20th Century-Fox, **C:** James Stewart, Jeff Chandler, Debra Paget, **R:** 7.20.1950

1954–1964: Europa, Hollywood
Désirée, **D:** Henry Koster, **P:** 20th Century-Fox, **C:** Marlon Brando, Merle Oberon, Jean Simmons, **R:** 11.16.1954, **E:** Oscar nomination
Una aventura de Gil Blas, **D:** René Jolivet/Ricardo Muñoz Suay, **P:** Vascos Films/Producciones Benito Perojo, **C:** Susana Canales, Georges Marchal, Fernando Rey, **R:** 4.6.1956, **E:** Only set design
Anastasia, **D:** Anatole Litvak, **P:** 20th Century-Fox, **C:** Ingrid Bergman, Yul Brynner, Helen Hayes, **R:** 12.13.1956
The Journey, **D:** Anatole Litvak, **P:** Alby Pictures/Metro-Goldwyn-Mayer, **C:** Yul Brynner, Deborah Kerr, **R:** 2.19.1959
The Four Horsemen of the Apocalypse, **D:** Vincente Minnelli, **P:** Metro-Goldwyn-Mayer, **C:** Charles Boyer, Glenn Ford, Yvette Mimieux, Ingrid Thulin, **R:** 2.7.1962
The Visit, **D:** Bernhard Wicki, **P:** 20th Century-Fox/Cinecittà/Deutsche Fox, **C:** Ingrid Bergman, Anthony Quinn, **R:** 5.6.1964, **E:** Oscar nomination

René Hubert in Archives and Collections

René Hubert put two of his costume designs in the exhibition *Das schweizerische Bühnenbild: Von Appia bis heute*, which the Swiss Society for Theatre Culture presented in several German-speaking cities from 1949 to 1954. Its director, Edmund Stadler, later accepted ninety sketches owned by Hubert – primarily for Hollywood films of the 1940s – for the Swiss Theatre Collection (now part of the SAPA Foundation) in Bern.

In 1974, just before his eightieth birthday, Hubert offered the rest of his archive to what was then the Museum Bellerive in Zurich for an exhibition. The museum declined, and so Walter Ludwig – Hubert's neighbor of many years at Finkenrain 7 in Zurich – is to thank that most of his estate has survived: without hesitation he purchased it from relatives of Hubert's partner, Georges Stamatiadis, after he passed away in 1978 and the apartment was cleared.

In 1998, Ludwig sold the estate, which included film stills, photographs of stage, fashion, et cetera, sketches for Swissair and many other items, to the collector Rolf Ramseier, who shortly thereafter passed on approximately one thousand film stills to the Cinémathèque suisse in Lausanne. This wealth of material formed the basis for the exhibition *René Hubert – The Clothes Make the Star,* which Andres Janser curated at the Museum für Gestaltung Zürich in 2021. After the exhibition closed, the museum accepted the objects relating to the stage, fashion and interior design, while the objects involving film (sketches, several hundred photographs, correspondence) went to the Cinémathèque suisse. Signed photographs and some other objects remained the possession of Ramseier.

In addition to the sketches at the SAPA Foundation and the Cinémathèque suisse, more than 300 have survived, most held by the Academy of Motion Picture Arts and Sciences, Los Angeles (Leonard Stanley Collection); Christian Esquevin Collection; the Brooklyn Museum Libraries, New York; La Cinémathèque Française, Paris; the University of Georgia, Hargrett Rare Book & Manuscript Library (Paris Music Hall Collection); the University of Texas at Austin, Harry Ransom Center (Gloria Swanson Papers, B. J. Simmons & Co. Costume Design Records); the Los Angeles County Museum of Art; the Deutsche Kinemathek, Berlin (Marlene Dietrich Collection); and the University of Cologne (Theater Research Collection).

Original film costumes are part of the collections of Joseph Davino, Nicholas Inglis and Larry McQueen.

Image Credits

Bibliothèque du Cinéma François Truffaut, Paris: pp. 126/127
bpk / Los Angeles County Museum of Art / Art Resource, NY: p. 94
British Film Institute, London: p. 13 (center right), pp. 116/117
Christian Esquevin Collection: pp. 80–81
The Cinema Museum, London: p. 105 (top)
Collecting Classic Hollywood: p. 27 (top right)
Collection Cinémathèque suisse, Lausanne: p. 9 (left and top), p. 11, p. 13 (top left and right), p. 17, p. 18 (bottom), p. 19, p. 21 (top), p. 23 (top left and bottom), p. 25 (top right, bottom left), p. 27 (top left), p. 33 (top left and right), p. 35 (top left and center, top right and center), pp. 42–43, pp. 45–48, pp. 54–55, p. 68, p. 70, pp. 72–73, p. 74 (top), p. 76 (bottom), p. 89, p. 93, p. 95, p. 99, p. 102, p. 104 (bottom), p. 106, p. 118–121, pp. 124–125, pp. 128–147, pp. 162–163, pp. 192–205, p. 213 (bottom left), p. 232, pp. 246/247
The Collection of John L. Coker III: p. 25 (bottom right)
The Collection of Motion Picture Costume Design: p. 105 (bottom)
Collection of the Swiss Museum of Transport, Lucerne: p. 211, pp. 230–231
Deutsche Kinemathek – Marlene Dietrich Collection, Berlin: p. 180
DFF – Deutsches Filminstitut & Filmmuseum, Frankfurt: p. 18 (top), p. 74 (bottom)
Duncan P. Schiedt Photograph Collection, Archives Center, National Museum of American History, Smithsonian Institution, Washington: p. 29 (bottom left and right), pp. 174–175
ETH Library Zurich, Image Archive/Stiftung Luftbild Schweiz: pp. 209–210, p. 213 (top left, top right and bottom right), pp. 214–215, p. 217
Historisches Archiv der Bally Schuhfabriken AG: p. 182 (bottom), p. 183 (bottom left, top right, center and bottom)
London Films: pp. 110–115
Angelo Luerti, Milan: p. 150 (top), p. 161
Mary Evans Picture Library, London: p. 155
Mary Evans/Jazz Age Club: pp. 164–165
Motion Picture and Television Photo Archive: p. 71
Museum für Gestaltung Zürich: p. 13 (bottom right), pp. 153–154, pp. 176/177, pp. 185–186, pp. 190–191, p. 219
Neue Zürcher Zeitung, May 28, 1958: p. 33 (bottom right)
The Paris Times, November 6, 1924: p. 9 (bottom)
Rolf Ramseier, Guntershausen: p. 14 (top left), p. 21 (bottom left and right), p. 69, p. 76 (top), p. 152 (top), p. 157, p. 181, p. 189, p. 212, pp. 221–228
SAPA Foundation, Swiss Archive of the Performing Arts, Bern: S. 31 (top right), p. 79, pp. 82–88, p. 90, p. 92, p. 103, p. 104 (top), p. 109, p. 159 (bottom)
Schweizer Textilien, no. 1, 1954: p. 184 (bottom)
Schweizerische Landesausstellung, ed. *Die Schweiz im Spiegel der Landesausstellung 1939*. Zurich: Atlantis Verlag, 1940: p. 183 (top left)
Shutterstock Inc.: p. 37
Sport im Bild, no. 27/28, 1922: p. 33 (bottom left)
Stadtarchiv Zürich: p. 159 (top), p. 187
Stiftung Deutsche Kinemathek, Berlin: p. 14 (top right), p. 15
Thomas Städeli, Dietikon: p. 229
Der Styl, no. 5/6, 1922: p. 184 (top)
Swissair-Gazette, no. 3, 1960: p. 218
Theriault's Doll Auctions, Annapolis: p. 23 (top right)
United Artists: pp. 51–53
United States Patent Office: p. 23 (bottom right)
Universal Pictures: p. 91
University of Cologne, Theaterwissenschaftliche Sammlung: p. 27 (bottom left and right), pp. 166–171
University of Bristol/ArenaPAL: p. 29 (top), p. 152 (bottom),
University of Georgia, Hargrett Library: p. 150 (bottom), pp. 172–173
The University of Texas at Austin, Harry Ransom Center, Gloria Swanson Papers: p. 13 (bottom left), pp. 57–65
The University of Texas at Austin, Harry Ransom Center, B. J. Simmons & Co. Costume Design Records: p. 25 (top left)
Universum Film: p. 14 (bottom)
Zürcher Illustrierte, no. 23, June 3, 1939: p. 182 (top)
20th Century-Fox: p. 31 (top, bottom left), p. 35 (bottom)

Index

Firms

20th Century-Fox 24, 28, 34, 39, 72–77, *72*, *130*, 152, 157, 233
Angels Costumes 98
Atelier Balenciaga 30, 77, 129, *130*, 180
B. J. Simmons 26, 28, 240
Bally 39, 182, *182–183*, 186, 218
Balmain 26
Barbara Karinska 26
Bulgari *188*
Christian Lacroix 98
Christoph Drecoll 74
Columbia 124, 216
Famous Players-Lasky/ Paramount *8*, 12, 38, 42, 69, *132*, 233
Films Sonores Tobis 12, 16, 20, 38, 233
Forster Willi 157, *157*
Fox Film 24, 38, 152, 233
Glentex *186*
Gloria Productions 42
Grieder 39, 182, 186, *187*
Heberlein *183*
Hills Brothers 68
House of Worth 26, 77
Hugo Baruch *26*, 38, *160*
International Air Transport Association 208
Jean Dessès 26
Jean Patou 26, 151
Jeanne Lanvin 98
Jeanne Paquin 26, 74
Jelmoli *32*, 39, 186
Karl Lagerfeld 98
London Films 24, 26, 38, 72, 98, 100, 103, 233
Metro-Goldwyn-Mayer (MGM) 12, 38, 69, 124, *124*, 233
Mustermesse Basel 32, 182
Nina Ricci 34, 77, 181, *188*
Pan American World Airways 216
Paramount Pictures 12, 48, 49
Pat Premo 30, 39, 184, *185*
Paul Poiret 74, 98
Pierre Cardin 98
RKO 124
Rose Valois 26
Schiaparelli 26
Stoffel 30, 32, 39, 157, *157*, 182, 184, *185*, 186, *188*
Les Studios Paramount 16, 20, *20*, 24, 37, 38, 181, 233, 234, *244*
Swissair 32, 39, 76, 207–210, *210*, *213*, 214, 216, *218–220*, 233, 240
Transcontinental & Western Air 32, 36, 216
United Air Lines 216
United Artists 42
Universum Film (Ufa) 12, 38, 152, *232*, 233
Warner Bros. 124
Yves Saint Laurent 98

Persons

Ackerman, Forrest J. 24, *24*
Adrian, *22*, 69, 124
Amann, Betty 12, *14*
D'Ambricourt, Adrienne *12*
Anderson, Mary *74*
André-ani, 69
Argyle, Pearl *118*
Armstrong, John 106
Aumond, Jean 151
Bachrach, Ernest A. 124, *124*
Balieff, Nikita *160*
Ball, Russell *10*, *124*
Bankhead, Tallulah *74*, 74–75
Banton, Travis 124
Barbier, Georges 68, *68*, 151
Bell, Marie *20*
Bendix, William *74*
Berchtold, Walter 209–210, 218
Bergman, Ingrid 30, *32*, 34, *34*, 36, *76*, 77, 129, *130*, 180–181, 186, 214, 233
Bertaux, Lucien 155
Best, Edna *152*
Bianchetti, Suzanne *42*
Bircher, Rudolf 208, 218
Biró, Lajos 100
Black, George 150, 155–156
Blanton, Jimmy *28*
Brahm, John *78*
Brando, Marlon 30, *30*, 34, 76
Browne, Louise 154, *154*
Brunelleschi, Umberto 150–151
Brynner, Yul 30, *32*
Bull, Clarence S. 124
Chanel, Coco 181
Chaplin, Charlie 16
Charell, Erik 20, 26, 36, 150–152, *160*
Chevalier, Maurice 151
Churchill, Winston 103
Clair, René 16, *71*, *78*, 98, 152, 233
Cody, Lew *12*
Corchi, Alberto 129, *130*
Cordy, Raymond *16*
Crain, Jeanne *78*
Crazy Gang, The 155
Cronyn, Hume *74*
Cummins, Peggy *72*, 75
Czettel, Ladislaus 151, 155
Damita, Lili 152
Dandridge, Dorothy 156
Daniels, Bebe 10
Darnell, Linda *30*, 75, 77, *78*
Davey, Leon 154, 156
Davy, Charles 103, 107
DeMille, Cecil B. 42, 48–49
Dennis, Harry 155
Dickson, Dorothy *153*, 154, *160*
Diener, Nelly *210*
Dietrich, Marlene 8, 22, 30, 38–39, *71*, 72, *78*, *99*, 100–102, 107, 180, *180–181*, 186, 207, 216, 218, 233
Donat, Robert *99*, 100–101, 107
Drain, Émile *42*
Douglas, Myrtle R. 24, *24*
Dudley, Countess of 30, 38
Dunne, Irene 216
Dürrenmatt, Friedrich 34, 181
Dwan, Allan *12*, 233
Egender, Karl 182
Ellington, Duke 28, *28*, 36, 150, 156, 157–158, *160*
Elliott, Madge *152*
Emney, Fred 154
Farmer, Michelle *48*, *133*
Feuillère, Edwige *20*
Feyder, Jacques 100
Fitzgerald, Geraldine *74*
Forbes, Madeleine *74*
Ford, Ruth *74*
Foster, Susanna 157
Franklin, Sidney *78*
Frayling, Christopher 106–107
Fretz, Robert 209
Fritsch, Willy 12, *16*
Fröhlich, Gustav 12, *14*
Furber, Douglas 156
Garbo, Greta 12
Gesmar, Charles 151
Gish, Dorothy *128*
Gish, Lilian 12, *14*
Golovine, Serge 158
Goulding, Edmund *78*
Grieder, Edgar 182
Grable, Betty 72–73, *73*
Graf, Herbert 158
Greer, Howard 32, 124, 216
Gyarmathy, Michel 155
Hale, Binnie 28, *152*, 153
Hardwicke, Cedric 107
Harper, Sue 103, 107
Hart, Janice 155
Harvey, Lilian 16, *16*
Haver, June *37*
Hayes, Helen 77
Head, Edith 48, 124
Hearne, Richard 154
Henson, Leslie 150, 154, *154*
Hepburn, Katharine 216
Hilton, James 101
Hitchcock, Alfred 74, 233
Hodiak, John *74*
Horning, Charles D. *24*
Howard, Leslie 100
Howard, Sydney 156
Hull, Henry *74*
Hurrell, George 124
Illéry, Pola 16, *16*
Irene, 32, 75, 124
Israel, Walter J. 157
Jackson, Potts 28, *28*, 158
Jeffries, Herb *28*
Jones, Jennifer 72
Jongh, Francis de *8*
Jouval, Gaby 182
Karlweis, Oskar 12, *16*
Kent, Duchess of 30, 38
Kenyon, Doris *68*
King, Henry *78*
Knox, Alexander *74*
Korda, Alexander 24, 26, 72, 98, 100, 102–103, 106–107, *108*, 152
Korda, Vincent 100, 107
Korda, Zoltan 100
Korngold, Erich 157
Koster, Henry *78*, *134*
Lasky, Jesse L. 69
Lawrence, John 155
Le Maire, Charles *37*, 72, 76–77, 233
Lehár, Franz 158
Leigh, Vivien 22, 30, 39, *100*, 101–107, *102–106*, *108*
Lemonnier, Meg 20, *20*
Lester, Edwin 150, 157
Linlithgow, Lady 30, 38
Lodwick, Keith 104, 107
Loper, Don 32, 216
Louis, Jean 75, 216
Louise, Ruth Harriet 124
Lubitsch, Ernst 74, 186, 233
Luick, Earl 72
Lynes, George Platt 124
May, Skillet 28, *28*
McCarey, Leo 49, 54
Mann, William J. 20, 36, 132
Maschwitz, Eric 150, 154
Massey, Raymond *24*, *118*
Maté, Rudolph *71*

Menzies, William Cameron 106, 118
Modot, Gaston 16, *16*
Monroe, Marilyn *128*
Moore, Owen *12*
Mozart, Wolfgang Amadeus 157, *157*
Munsel, Patrice 158
Nelson, Paul 12
Novello, Ivor 20, 36, *153*, 153–155
O'Brian, Frank 155
Oberon, Merle 98, 100, 103, 107, 129, *133*, 233
Offenbach, Jacques 152
Olivier, Laurence 103, *104–105*, 108
Orczy, Baroness 100
Pearce, Vera 156
Perret, Léonce 10, 69
Peter, Charlotte 207, 216, 218
Petit, Valentine 10
Piguet, Robert 182
Pommer, Erich 12, 152
Préjean, Albert 16, *16*
Preminger, Otto 75, *78*, 233
Premo, Pat 30, 39, *184–185*
Queensberry, Marchioness of 106
Quinn, Anthony *34*, *76*
Rambova, Natacha 68, *68*
Ramseier, Rolf 186, 234, 240, 244, 245
Rasimi, Bénédicte 68, 150–151, 233
Reader, Ralph 150, 153, *160*
Reinhardt, Max 157
Revolg, Estelle 155
Richardson, Ralph 107
Riscoe, Arthur 156
Robey, George 152
Robson, Flora 103, *106*
Romney, George 105
Rózsa, Miklós 100
Rühmann, Heinz 12, *16*
Sagan, Leontine *160*
Schneider, Max *220*
Schröder, Ernst *76*
Schuh, Gotthard *182*
Schuppisser, Wilhelm 182
Scott, Margaretta 106–107
Scrimali, Fortunato *34*, 181, *188*
Selten, Morton *106*
Shanks, Alec 155
Sharaff, Irene 75
Shephard, Firth 154
Shubert, Lee 38, 68, 150–151, 233
Simmons, Jean 30, *30*, 34, 76, *78*, 129, *134*
Stamatiadis, Georges 22, 233, 240
Stein, Fred *55*
Stern, Ernst 151–152, 155
Sternberg, Josef von 101
Stevenson, Edward 75
Stewart, Sophie *118*
Stockfeld, Betty 20
Strauss, Johann 157, 158, *159*
Stroeva, Dora 151
Stroheim, Erich von 44, 48
Swanson, Gloria 8, 10, *10*, 12, *12*, *26*, 30, 36, 38, 41–42, *42*, 44–45, *45*, *47*, 48–51, *48*, *51*, *54–56*, 68–69, 73, 76–77, *124*, *128*, *133*, 152, 180, 181, 186, 233
Tabori, Paul 100, 107
Tacchella, Jean-Charles 98, 107
Temple, Shirley 20, 22, *22*, 24, 36, 38, 70, *70*, 77, 187
Tobler, Jakob *219*
Tree, Dolly 151
Valentino, Rudolph 10, 68, *68*
Vandamm, Florence *8*, *132*
Veidt, Conrad 102, *102*
Verdi, Giuseppe 158
Villiers, Kenneth *24*, *118*
Vilpelle, Madeleine 151
Wagner, Robert *48*, *133*
Walling, William *71*
Ward, Billy *78*
Ware, Pans *28*, *28*
Wells, H. G. 106–7
Wicki, Bernhard 34, 132
Wieder, Achille *219*
Wilde, Cornel *30*, 75
Wilder, Billy 45, 48–49, 132
Wilson, Lois 69, *69*
Wimperis, Arthur 100
Wolgensinger, Michael *218*
Wyler, William 103
Zamora, José de 151
Zanuck, Darryl F. 34
Zumsteg, Gustav 180

Works

À nous la liberté 16, *16*, 38
The Affairs of Anatol 42
Airport 1975 44
Alles neu 156
An Alle 8, 26, 38, *150*, 151
Asphalt 12, *14*
L'Auberge du Cheval Blanc *150*, 152
Balalaika 154
The Best Years of Our Lives 75
Careless Rapture 153, *153*, *160*
Catherine the Great 103
Centennial Summer 75, *78*, *128*
La chance *20*
La Chauve-Souris 158, *160*
Cinderella *152*, 153
The Coast of Folly 38, *42*, *45*
Così fan tutte 157, *157*
Crest of a Wave 153
Curly Top *22*, 24, 38, 70, *70*, 187
Dark Journey 30, 38, 100, 102, *102*
Darling You 155
De Toutes les Couleurs 150
Désirée 30, *30*, 32, 34, 39, 76, *78*, 128, 132, *133–134*
The Divorce of Lady X 98, 107
Don't Change Your Husband 42
Die Drei von der Tankstelle 12, *16*, 22, 38
Eve 156
Father Takes a Wife 39, 54, *55*, *124*, *128*
Fire over England 38, 98, 100, *100*, 103, 106–107, *106*
The Flame of New Orleans 16, 39, *71*, 72, *78*
Die Fledermaus 157–158
Floodlight 155
Footlight Serenade 73
Forever Amber 30, *30*, 39, *72*, 75–77, *78*
The Four Feathers 100
The Ghost Goes West 16, 98, 100, 106–107
Gilda 75
Going Greek 154
Gone With the Wind 103–105
Hokuspokus 16, 38, *232*
The Humming Bird 10
Il est charmant 20, *20*
Im weissen Rössl 20, 26, *26*, 38, 152, *160*
Indiscreet 30, 38, 49, *51*
It's a Wonderful Life 75
Jump for Joy 28, *28*, 30, 36, 156, 158, *160*
June Love 151
Kissing Time 151
Knight Without Armour 38, 72, *99*, 100–101
Lifeboat 39, 74, *74*
London Rhapsody 155, *155*
Love 12, 38, *78*
The Love of Sunya 10, *10*, 38, 45, *45*, *47*, *124*
The Love Song 8, 152
Madame Sans-Gêne 10, 36, 38, 42, *42*, 44, 69, 72, 76, 152, 233
The Merry Widow 158
Metropolis 12
Modern Times 16
Monsieur Albert 20, *20*, 38
Monsieur Beaucaire 10, 38, 68–69, *68*, 151
Music in the Air 38, 54, *55*
My Darling Clementine 39, 75
Naughty Marietta 157
New Faces 155
Nuit de Folies 152
Our Little Girl 24, 38, 70
Paprika 154
Pelissier's Follies of 1938 156
Pin Up Girl *73*
The Postman Always Rings Twice 75
Princess Virtue 151
The Private Life of Don Juan 103
The Private Life of Henry VIII 103
Quatorze Juillet 16, 38
Queen Kelly 44, 48
La revue trés excitante 8, 151
Rise and Shine 28, *28*, 107, *152*, *153*
Rosalinda 157
Running Riot 154
Sadie Thompson 42
The Scarlet Empress 101
The Scarlet Pimpernel 100
Sitting Pretty 156
The Song of Bernadette 72
Sous les toits de Paris 16, 38
Stage Struck 38, *47*
Sunset Boulevard *45*, 48–49, *48*, 54, 132, *133*
Sweet Rosie O'Grady 72
Swing Along 154, *154*
Swiss Echoes *157*, 158
The Temporary Widow 16, 38, *232*
That Hamilton Woman 39, 98, 100, 103–104, *103–105*, 106–107, *108*
Théâtre de la Chauve-Souris 38, 151, *160*
Things to Come 24, *24*, 38, 100, *106*, 106–107, *118*, 132
The Three Musketeers 157
La Traviata 158
Topaze 20, 38
Tu seras Duchesse 20, 38
Une nuit à l'hotel 20
Der verlorene Faden 156, *182*
Vive la Femme! 8, 151
The Visit *32*, 34, *34*, 39, *76*, 77, 132, 180–181, 186, *188*, 214, 233
What a Widow! 12, *12*, *26*, 30, 38, *47*
Why Change Your Wife? 42
Wild Oats 156
Wilson 39, 74, *74*, *78*
The Wind 12, *14*, 38
Wuthering Heights 103
Ziegfeld Follies of 1922 151

Authors

Andres Janser, freelance historian of film, design and architecture, Zurich. Former editor of the periodical *archithese* and research fellow at the Institute of History and Theory of Architecture, ETH Zurich. After that he was the curator at the Museum für Gestaltung Zürich from 2003 to 2021 and completed more than two dozen projects, some of which were shown internationally. The latest was the exhibition *René Hubert: The Clothes Make the Star* (2021).

His publications and exhibitions include *Hans Richter: New Living. Architecture, Film, Space* (2001), *Trickraum/Spacetricks* (2005), *Chris Marker: Abschied vom Kino* (2008), *Corporate Diversity: Swiss Graphic Design and Advertising by Geigy 1940–1970* (2009), *Bewegte Schrift* (2011), *Verbrechen lohnt sich: Der Kriminalfilm* (2012), *Animierte Wunderwelten*/Animated Wonderworlds (2015) and *SBB CFF FFS* (2019).

Elisabeth Bronfen, cultural and literary scholar, professor at the University of Zurich. (Co)author of *Nur über ihre Leiche: Tod, Weiblichkeit und Ästhetik* (1994/2004) and *Diva: Eine Geschichte der Bewunderung* (1994).

Roland Fischer-Briand, head of the photography collection at the Austrian Theatre Museum, Vienna. Former head of the photography collection at Cinémathèque suisse, Lausanne. Author of texts on film stills, such as in *Film-Stills: Fotografien zwischen Werbung, Kunst und Kino* (2016).

Angelo Luerti, design historian, Milan. Author of *Non solo Erté = Not only Erté: Costume Design for the Paris Music Hall, 1918–1940* (2005).

Deborah Nadoolman Landis, founding director of the David C. Copley Center of Costume Design, University of California, Los Angeles. Author/editor of *Dressed: A Century of Hollywood Costume Design* (2006), *Hollywood Sketchbook: A Century of Costume Illustration* (2012) and *Hollywood Costume* (2013).

Rolf Ramseier, collector of Swiss autographs, Guntershausen. Owned René Hubert's estate for many years.

Amy Sargeant, assistant professor at Fordham University, London. (Co)author of *British Historical Cinema: The History, Heritage and Costume Film* (2002) and *British Cinema: A Critical History* (2005).

Katharina Tietze, professor at Zurich University of the Arts. Coeditor of *Mode und Bewegung: Beiträge zur Geschichte und Theorie der Kleidung* (2013) and *Über Schuhe: Zur Geschichte und Theorie der Fussbekleidung* (2016).

> René Hubert at his studio at Les Studios Paramount in Joinville, near Paris, 1932

Acknowledgments

We would like to thank the family of René Hubert and most importantly Felix Baumer, who provided access to Hubert's unpublished memoirs. Rolf Ramseier, who preserved the estate for many years, Christian Wapp and Céline G. Arzatian supplied valuable input.

The authors of the book's contributions embarked on this complex adventure with a great deal of passion, and important material was made available by numerous archives and collections.

We thank the institutions, foundations and firms whose generous support made this book possible.

Andres Janser/Lars Müller

Kanton St. Gallen Kulturförderung/Swisslos
Kanton Thurgau/Lotteriefonds
Kanton Zürich Fachstelle Kultur
Ortsbürgergemeinde St. Gallen
Ria & Arthur Dietschweiler Stiftung
Heinrich Hössli Stiftung
Steinegg Stiftung
Mary und Max Steinmann-Stiftung des Rotary Clubs St. Gallen
Hans und Wilma Stutz Stiftung
Dr. Fred Styger Stiftung
TISCA Tischhauser Stiftung
Akris
Filtex AG

René Hubert

The Man Who
Dressed Film Stars
and Airplanes

Editor: Andres Janser
Authors: Elisabeth Bronfen, Roland Fischer-Briand, Andres Janser, Angelo Luerti, Deborah Nadoolman Landis, Rolf Ramseier, Amy Sargeant, Katharina Tietze
Translations (G>E) and copyediting: Steve Wilder
Proofreading: Elissa Sweet
Project coordination: Marius Wenger
Design: Integral Lars Müller/Lars Müller and Esther Butterworth
Cover design: Integral Lars Müller/Lars Müller and Hanna Welzel
Production: Esther Butterworth
Printing, binding and lithography: DZA Druckerei zu Altenburg, Germany
Paper: Arctic Volume White 1.1, 130 gsm

Lars Müller Publishers is supported by the Swiss Federal Office of Culture with a structural contribution for the years 2021–2024.

Lars Müller Publishers
Zurich, Switzerland
www.lars-mueller-publishers.com

ISBN 978-3-03778-700-7 (English)
ISBN 978-3-03778-699-4 (German)

Distributed in North America by ARTBOOK | D.A.P.
www.artbook.com

Printed in Germany